The
First Landfall

Historic Lighthouses of
Newfoundland and Labrador

David J. Molloy

BREAKWATER

BREAKWATER
100 Water Street
P.O. Box 2188
St. John's, NF
A1C 6E6

Cover Credit: "Blue Bank", oil on canvas by artist Tara
            Bryan. Reproduced with the kind
            permission of *Christina Parker Fine Art*,
            St. John's, NF.
Cover inset photo: David Molloy

Canadian Cataloguing in Publication Data
  Molloy, David, 1954-
    The first landfall
    ISBN 1-55081-096-0

    1. Lighthouses—Newfoundland. 2. Lighthouse
    keepers—Newfoundland. I. Title.
VK1027.N5M65   1994   387.1'55'09718   C94-950074-7

Dedication

This book is dedicated to the Sheppards of Fort Amherst, the Cantwells of Cape Spear, the Whites of Cape Bonavista, the Hewitts of Cape Pine, the Wyatts of Point Amour, the Myricks of Cape Race, the Costellos of Ferryland Head, the Cambells of Cape Norman and all the other keepers and their families who kept the lights on our coasts for one hundred and eighty years.

And to my daughter Tara and my son Matthew in hopes that they will come to know and love this place as much as I do.

Acknowledgements

I wish to acknowledge the able assistance of the staff of several institutions including the Centre for Newfoundland Studies at Memorial Univiersity, the Provincial Archives of Newfoundland and Labrador and the Canadian Coast Guard in St. John's. Without their help this book would not have been possible.

The many photographs found in this book have been reproduced with permission of the Ministeries of Transportation Canada and Supply and Services Canada, March 1994, the Centre for Newfoundland Studies and the Provincial Archives of Newfoundland and Labrador.

Several engravings have been used in this book. They have been obtained from a collection of scenes published in Charles DeVolpi's *Newfoundland: A Pictoral Record* (1972).

I wish to thank a number of special people who helped me as I wrote this book, including: Bruce Stacey, a retired lighhouse enthusiast, who single-handedly has saved many of the photographs, artifacts and memories of a hundred years of Newfoundland lighthouse history; the present day keepers of the lights and Mrs. Margaret Cantwell, wife of the late Frank Cantwell, who told me of her memories of keeping the Lights; Dr. Malcolm MacLeod, Professor of History at Memorial University, who gave me some good advice when I needed it; Mrs. Theresa MacDonald, of the Cape North Historical Society in Cape Breton; Mrs. Margaret Linthorne, curator of the Bonavista Museum; Alf Power; Cindy Gibbons; Bruce MacTavish; Anne Marceau and Michael Burzynsky and later Tod Boland who told me about the orchids of Cape Norman; my friend Sue Manuel for her kind editoral assistance and to my wife Marilyn, who kept my mug filled and was my silent supporter through all those long winter months.

Contents

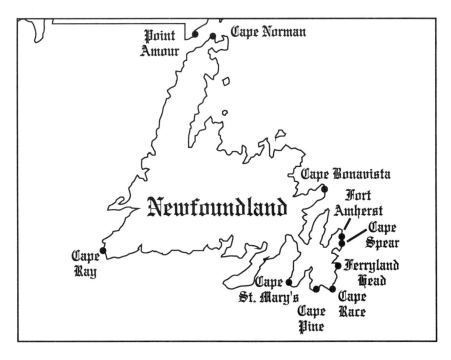

Prologue

There's something thrilling about standing on a rocky point of land beside a raging sea. Magnificent swells roll over a jagged shoal offshore. Breakers build high before crashing in a white maelstrom at our feet. It is here that the land meets the sea in a sort of dynamic balance. For some, this place holds an uncommon fascination.

The last rays of the setting sun pierce ragged storm clouds. Watching there, we brace against the growing Northeasterly gale. What must it be like to be on board a boat on a night like this? Lost out there in the growing darkness, imagine a storm-tossed ship skirting the outer reef. What chill ran through their hearts on hearing the boom of these breakers?

Behind us, the stark form of the lighthouse flashes its reassuring light out into the night, guiding them in their passage. It marks this threshold between land and sea as a place which man has tamed. The lighthouse has the power to claim a part of the landscape for itself. Its unique shape is set apart from the marine environment. While the lighthouse dominates the headland visually, it dominates our imaginations as well.

Since John Cabot's day, nearly five hundred years ago, men have been drawn to the riches of our fishing grounds. Back then explorers and fishermen in sailing ships plied our coastline. Later, with the growth of the fishery, warships came from many countries to try to gain control of this rocky Island. Finally, tall ships laden with goods from around the world began supplying the oldest colony of Great Britain. These ships departed again with their holds filled with salt cod. Given the caprices of the North Atlantic, many ships were wrecked here in those early years; uncounted men and ships were lost on our shores. By the beginning of the nineteenth century, a cry arose from the merchants for a system of lights to help mariners navigate along this treacherous coastline.

The idea was not new; navigational lights have existed since ancient times in the Middle East, the Holy Roman Empire and "enlightened" Europe and Britain. The first lighthouse in North America was built off Boston Harbour in 1716. Sixteen years later, a French Governor built the first Canadian lighthouse at the entrance to Louisbourg Harbour. Local merchants commissioned Newfoundland's first lighthouse at Fort Amherst in the entrance to St. John's harbour in 1813. So began the long history of the Newfoundland lights, each lighthouse having a story to tell, each story—a testament to dedication and perseverance of the keepers confronted with our extraordinary marine environment.

In the nineteenth century, the Colonial government began a process to find the best sites for the Newfoundland lighthouses. Young surveyors travelled the coastline searching for those capes and points of land which were the highest and thrust the furthest out into the sea. They created a series of lighthouse stations on sites which were, and still are, some of the wildest places in the world. While many of the lights are automatic now, the indomitable spirit of keepers still inhabits them. When you visit them, you may be transported back to the time when they were first manned. These lighthouses are truly evocative places, they speak not just of the Victorian materials from which they are made, but also of the intangible rhythms, spirits, and dreams of people who inhabited them. These sites are a tiny piece of the real world, yet they were made to seem like an entire world for the keeper and his family. Unknowingly, their designers expressed an attitude about life, striving to push the bounds of what was known and what was possible.

A number of magnificent coastal sites throughout Newfoundland were developed in the mid-nineteenth century. For one hundred years, the Inspectors of Lighthouses published a lucid series of Annual Reports for the Newfoundland House of Assembly. These Reports chronicled the development of the lighthouse system in Newfoundland; they have formed the basis for this book. They detailed the construction and operation of our finest stone and iron lighthouses. The information is complete with copies of original drawings, photographs and written descriptions of the work.

The lighthouses were built to withstand the ferocious Newfoundland climate. They have been well maintained and many remain much as they were during the time of their construction. Given the inaccessibility of these sites, the Colonial government was forced to cut through the barrens and highlands to reach these far-flung places. These roads are still used today, and for the most part remain quite passable.

Information about our oldest lighthouses is scattered throughout countless documents. Many of the retired keepers can still relate amazing stories about their lives at the stations. It is surprising that there has never been an effort to piece this information together. This is the goal of this book, to tell the story of these evocative places that link us to our past. Indirectly, these lighthouses connect us to those who tried to wrestle a living from the grey sea so many years ago.

For those who are interested in exploring some of Newfoundland's most hauntingly beautiful, most historic marine sites, the chapters that follow may help in that quest. For anyone who visits these coastal sites, they surely will agree that our historic lighthouses are some of the most memorable places in our province.

The System of Newfoundland Lights

"Newfoundland occupies nearly the same position in the new world that Britain does in the old. Stretching far out into the Atlantic, the nearest part of North America to Europe, she became the half-way house, the stepping stone between the two continents. By her shores passed all the great discoverers and the flowing tide of European emigration which peopled North America.. . . . ."

from *A History of Newfoundland* by Judge David W. Prowse

The story of the Newfoundland lights begins after the War of 1812 in what must have seemed a lull in the storm. For over one hundred and fifty years, two powerful European nations had been engaged in a fight over who controlled the lucrative Newfoundland fishery. During those years, both Britain and France sent stern military Governors to rule over the simple folk who fished there each summer. By the end of the eighteenth century, Britain managed to wrestle the rocky Island away from France.

It was not until after the war with the Americans that a peace of sorts settled on the rocky coasts and sheltered bays. It was a peace that would be quickly broken by the thunder of the Industrial Revolution and the winds of democracy that were swept in from across the Atlantic

Ocean. Grudgingly, the military Governors were forced to loosen the strict controls that they had placed on the coastal communities of Newfoundland. These were excellent years for the fishery. Thousands of English and Irish immigrants flooded into St. John's and the many outport communities scattered around the Avalon peninsula and the northeastern coast of the Island. Since the seventeenth century, a middle class of fish merchants, tradesmen and professionals used the harbour of St. John's as a base for their operations. Most came from an area of England around Devonshire and Dorsetshire known as *the West Country*. At the beginning of the nineteenth century, they formed the business elite in St. John's. These men were quite familiar with their own country's recent efforts to reform the British Parliament. With reform in mind, they began to voice their opinions on the affairs of the new Colony. They were confronted by the rough justice of a military Governor named Sir Charles Hamilton. His adherence to maritime law and his restrictions on their right to own property angered them. They wanted a Governor who was more in tune with their needs and concerns, able to respond to the social and economic issues facing the Island Colony. They needed a government which could begin the task of developing a system of public works and services that could support their business interests.

In 1825, a new Governor, Sir Thomas Cochrane arrived in St. John's. Over the next ten years, he would change the face of public affairs in Newfoundland. Cochrane realized that many of the people's concerns were justified, particularly with respect to developing infrastructure in the new Colony. He quickly moved to establish the first road building program on the Island, at the same time supporting a relief system for the poor by employing them on these projects. Through his encouragement, the Supreme Court of Newfoundland became a reality. Cochrane ordered the construction of a number of public buildings in St. John's including a children's orphanage and the town's first fire hall. He also ordered a new residence for himself to be built on Military Road. This beautiful mansion built of local red sandstone is still used as the residence of the present day Lieutenant Governor.

At the beginning of his tenure, Governor Cochrane was pressed by the business elite to grant a Constitution to the Colony, giving the people the power to govern themselves. While Representative governments existed in a number of other British North American Colonies, Cochrane had to be convinced that the unruly Newfoundlanders were capable of managing their own affairs.

In 1831, they finally persuaded him and he made way for Representative government. This system of government included a House of Assembly which consisted of fifteen Members elected from nine Districts located around the Island. What confused the arrangement was a

10

separate Upper House, working as a sort of Senate. It was known as a Legislative or Executive Council and was made up of *appointed* officials who were to advise the Governor on matters of State. Right from the start, they were split along religious lines. The House and the Executive would be constantly at odds with each other over the administration of the Colony. The first general election in Newfoundland took place in 1832. This would be an inauspicious start to one hundred years of controversy, argument and even violence in Newfoundland politics.

On January 1, 1833, the first session of the House of Assembly opened in St. John's. In Governor Cochrane's *Speech from the Throne*, he set before the House an impressive list of legislation and public works that his new Government intended to proceed with. He included such civilizing ideas as a start to town planning and the establishment of new schools and roads. He also proposed the establishment of a police force for the outport communities and a savings bank for the common people.

In that opening address, Governor Cochrane introduced the idea of establishing a system of navigational aids to ring the treacherous coastline of Newfoundland. This was not a new idea to the merchants of St. John's for they had been after Cochrane to establish such a system of lights for years. They had felt so strongly about the need to light the entrance of St. John's harbour that they erected the first light there on their own in 1813. For twenty years the light operated on the donations from these same merchants.

The idea of a system of lights operated by the new government was just what the merchants needed. They had been trying to develop trade links between Britain and North America, and were at the mercy of the vagaries of a cruel North Atlantic Ocean. The unlit, often foggy coastline was taking an increasing toll on the vessels that passed through New-foundland waters. Not only would these lights warn mariners of dangerous reefs and hazardous capes but, more importantly, their individual and distinctive light characteristics would aid navigators in fixing their positions as they passed along the dangerous coasts.

The merchants were "preaching to one of the converted" when it came to Thomas Cochrane. Before his appointment as Governor, he served over forty years in the Royal Navy. As a master mariner, he had come to know and depend on the twenty lighthouses that operated around the coasts of England and Wales at the time. A Crown corporation known as *Trinity House* operated these early English lights. Originally chartered by Henry VII in 1514, Trinity House was charged with improving British navigation and commerce. Later, it was given the task of establishing and maintaining lighthouses on English coasts. The Commissioners, or *Brethren* as they called themselves, were appointed to control the activities of Trinity House. The Brethren were really the same merchants and businessmen who had a vested interest in making the coastline safe for shipping. To pay for the construction and maintenance of the English Lighthouses, the government imposed an annual tax on every vessel using an English harbour. A similar arrangement existed in Scotland; there it was known as the *Northern Lighthouse Board*. The government in Lower Canada had established a similar corporation in 1805. They called it *Quebec Trinity House*. Initially, they were responsible for "the improvement of Navigation between Quebec and Montreal" but by mid century, their mandate broadened to include all of the Gulf of St. Lawrence.

The new government in St. John's chose to use this British approach as their model for establishing their own Board. On June 12, 1834, "The Act for the Establishment of Lighthouses" received Royal Assent and the *Newfoundland Lighthouse Board* became a reality. This institution in its various forms would be responsible for the establishment and operation of the lighthouses in Newfoundland for one hundred years.

That summer, Thomas Bennett was appointed the first Chairman and Chief Inspector for the Board. The forty-six year old businessman from Shaftesbury, Dorsetshire, had immigrated to Newfoundland in the 1820s. He and his brother Charles started the Bennett Brewing Company at Riverhead, in the west end of St. John's, making a popular ale known as *Dominion*. They must have made quite a success of it, because Dominion Ale can still be purchased in Newfoundland liquor stores today. Thomas Bennett had been a supporter of Representative government; when the first General Elections took place he ran and was elected as the Member for Twillingate and Fogo Island. He later became the Speaker of the House and was also appointed to the Board of Control which regulated road construction.

Bennett, together with the other Commissioners, quickly took action to improve the situation for mariners approaching St. John's harbour. They ordered the construction of the lighthouse at Cape Spear marking the entrance to St. John's Bay. They contracted Robert Stevenson, the Lighthouse Engineer from Edinburgh, to make recommendations about developing a lighthouse there. Stevenson had begun his career as the Chief Lighthouse Engineer with Northern Lighthouse Board in Scotland. He was responsible for the design and construction of the famous lighthouse at Bell Rock (Inchcape). This amazing stone tower was built on a submerged reef that thrust out into the shipping lanes of the Firth of Forth on the east coast of Scotland. This engineering feat was important because it demonstrated that lighthouses could be built just about anywhere in the world. Robert Stevenson and later, his sons Allan, David and Thomas Stevenson, all would have long and illustrious careers working with the Newfoundland Lighthouse Board. As their engineers, they guided the design of many of the Newfoundland lighthouses through to the end of the nineteenth century. Interestingly,

Thomas's son, Robert Louis Stevenson, would eclipse them all. He became the author of such well known sea adventures as *Treasure Island* and *Kidnapped*.

In 1836, the Commissioners ordered the second lighthouse to be built on Harbour Grace Island; this lighthouse had a similar design as the one at Cape Spear. They hired a forty-three year old Englishman from Southampton to be the keeper there. A mechanic by trade, Robert Oke was an excellent choice for the isolated lighthouse situated on the rocky island that lay just off the entrance to Harbour Grace harbour. For years, he had worked with several fish merchants in Harbour Grace and knew the coastal waters of Conception Bay very well. Later that year, he and his wife Ann and their sons moved out to the station. Thus began the career of an English gentleman who probably would have the greatest impact on the development of lighthouses in Newfoundland.

On the advice of his Secretary, Ambrose Shea, Chairman Bennett made the final decision on the site for a lighthouse at Cape Bonavista in 1842. The following year, he sent Oke out to oversee the installation of the light mechanism at the Cape Bonavista lighthouse. That same year, Bennett made the first of many requests to the House of Assembly to build a lighthouse at Cape Pine. This would not be accomplished for another nine years; not before the British Admiralty and Trinity House in London stepped in to help build it. In 1851, while the Cape Race lighthouse was under construction, the sixty-three year old Chairman resigned from the Lighthouse Board. He was appointed as a Magistrate in St. John's where he remained until he retired in 1870.

Politically, these were tumultuous years for the young Colony. Governor Cochrane had been replaced first by Sir Henry Prescott and later by Sir John Harvey. Neither could do much to hold the fractious Lower and Upper Houses of the government together. Animosity grew quickly and there was violence and bloodshed. They tried amalgamating the two Houses for a six-year period in the 1840s, only to return to Representative government in 1848.

It was a new Governor, Sir John LeMarchant, who appointed Nicholas Stabb as the second Chairman and Chief Inspector for the Lighthouse Board in 1851. Stabb, a native of Torquay on the coast of Devonshire, England, was another successful merchant in St. John's. He was a member of a well known West Country mercantile family that had been trading in Newfoundland for two hundred years. His reform minded brother, Dr. Henry Stabb, is credited with having founded the Waterford Hospital at Palk's Cottage on Waterford Bridge Road several years before.

Nicholas Stabb's tenure as Chairman of the Lighthouse Board was brief. After a divisive public debate, the Colony was granted Responsible government in 1855. This was what many had been fighting for years, a government in which all the Members were elected. It meant that all levels of government, including the Boards and later Departments would be directly responsible to the people of Newfoundland. The civilian-controlled Lighthouse Board was dissolved and replaced with the Lighthouse Service. The Lighthouse Service became the largest branch of the Board of Works. An elected Member of the House was appointed by the Prime Minister as Chairman.

Nicholas Stabb resigned that summer but remained in public life pursuing a career in politics. In 1860, he was elected and served as a Member of the House of Assembly in two successive Conservative administrations.

While the political control of the Service had been settled, the government still needed someone to advise the Chairman. They needed someone who had a keen understanding of the technology and an appreciation of the day to day operation of the lighthouses themselves. They chose Robert Oke. He had operated Harbour Grace Island lighthouse for more than a decade. After a short illness, he retired, leaving the station to one of his sons. His wife Ann was ill and they chose to move into St. John's. A couple of years later, she passed away. At the ripe old age of 62, Oke had the experience, interest and, it seems, the free time to devote himself to a new career as Chief Inspector for the Newfoundland Lighthouse Service.

Over the next twenty-five years, Robert Oke would become the best known, most respected of the Inspectors to hold the position. He designed and built six lighthouses in his first six years as Inspector. They were built in the most inaccessible locations in the Colony. Oke began with the construction of the Green Island lighthouse at the entrance to Catalina harbour. He quickly followed with the lighthouse on Offer Wadham Island marking the entrance to Hamilton Sound - the eastern channel to New World Island and Twillingate. Dodding Head lighthouse at the entrance to Burin harbour came next, followed by the Baccalieu Island lighthouse at the very tip of the Avalon Peninsula. He commissioned Cape St. Mary's lighthouse in 1860, marking the high headland separating St. Mary's Bay and Placentia Bay. Later came the lighthouse on Brunette Island in Fortune Bay off Harbour Breton. Finally, he ordered the construction of the Ferryland Head lighthouse located half way down the Southern Shore. This last lighthouse would not be completed until after he died.

In each case, Oke had the responsibility of recommending the final location for the lighthouse station. Their locations reflect the extent of settlement and commerce that existed in Newfoundland at the time. His decisions were fraught with controversy, for the inhabitants of every cove and harbour wanted the lighthouse station built near their community. Oke believed that lighthouses were chiefly navigational aids.

14

This idea came across in his 1866 Annual Report to the House of Assembly:

> As to the best site for a light on the coast referred to, the opinions, as might be expected, are conflicting according to the value which is set on the various elements and interest which enter into, and then bias the enquiry. In such cases, what should be done is carefully to weigh all the circumstances of the locality, and *give that site the preference which gives the greatest balance of interest to Navigation*. The best position for a Sea Light should never be rejected for the sake of the more immediate benefit of some neighbouring Port. And the interest of Navigation, as well, as the true welfare of the Port itself, will be better served by first placing your Sea Light where it ought to be, and as your means will afford, adding, on a smaller scale, such subsidiary lights to the entrance of such Ports as are most frequented and regarded as Harbours of Refuge.

Robert Oke was quite a promoter of their system of lighthouses. In 1860, the St. John's Board of Trade needed to inform British, American and Canadian business interests of the great improvements that had been made on the east coast of the Island. Inspector Oke cooperated by having a set of drawings prepared showing the lighthouses that he was operating at the time. They were beautifully rendered and were complete with a written description of their light characteristics and operation. These drawings represent one of the best "snapshots" of our oldest Newfoundland lighthouses. Perhaps the English architect John Nevill prepared them. Nevill had been working in St. John's since the early 1850s. By 1865, he was hired as the Inspector of Public Buildings for the Board of Works. Although it was not really his responsibility, he seemed to have an interest in the lighthouses. He began to travel with Oke, who was by now in his early seventies.

On the mainland, the course was set for the confederation of a number of the British North American Provinces. With the union of Upper and Lower Canada in 1841, the Canadian Board of Works took over responsibility for the construction and maintenance of lighthouses in the Gulf of St. Lawrence. The Quebec Trinity House remained in an advisory capacity to the Board. It was Quebec Trinity House that recommended the construction of the lighthouse at Point Amour on the southern coast of Labrador in 1850 and on Belle Isle a couple of years later.

In 1860, Trinity House in Quebec City ordered their Chief Engineer, Robert Page, out into the Gulf of St. Lawrence to survey the region for new lighthouse sites. Page's recommendations included several possible sites along what was called the *French Shore* of Newfoundland. A hundred years before, the fishing rights along the northwestern coast of the Island had been ceded to France. As no Newfoundlanders fished or had business interests there, the Newfoundland government up to that point did not feel it necessary to erect lighthouses there. Canadian shipping on the other hand was greatly affected by lack of lights in the region. By the mid-nineteenth century, Quebec Trinity House began to plan for the construction of several lighthouses along the French Shore. They dutifully corresponded with the Newfoundland government requesting their approval of the final sites. It was Robert Oke who crossed swords with them over the proper location of a lighthouse for the southwest corner of the Island. The argument went on for over a decade and wasn't resolved until after Robert Oke died. They eventually decided to build the lighthouse at Cape Ray, overruling Oke's recommendations. Several others were built at the same time at New Ferrolle, Cape Norman and Point Riche. In 1867, the British North America Act proclaimed the Dominion of Canada. The following year legislation established the Department of Marine and Fisheries in Ottawa. This Canadian Department took over the job of planning, building and maintaining lighthouses in the Gulf of St. Lawrence.

Robert Oke never actually retired from the Lighthouse Service. He passed away in September, 1870 at seventy-seven years of age. He was buried in the old Anglican Cemetery in St. John's next to his wife. Their quiet gravesite on the crest of the cemetery hill looks out past Quidi Vidi Lake toward the open sea.

John Nevill became the new Inspector, and while he was responsible for many important improvements, he may not have had the same zeal that his predecessor took to the job. His duties as Lighthouse Inspector were added to his other duties as Inspector of Public Buildings. It seems that he was irked by the fact that the Legislature never appreciated the extra work that it entailed. In his 1878 Report, he complained, "These increases have added largely to the care, responsibility and labour of my office, and I beg to submit that the amount of my salary is an inadequate renumeration for my services, and to express a hope for favourable consideration during the approaching session of the Legislature." It appears that he never got the financial satisfaction that he was looking for. In 1886, as he neared the end of his years as Inspector, he wrote bitterly, "I beg respectfully to submit that my salary is altogether too small for the amount and kind of work performed, the latter being....that of an expert as Architect and Engineer, particularly in the designing of many new works executed of late." Perhaps he never fully realized the contribution that he made to the lives of countless mariners and their families. Hopefully he did, for the simple gratification of financial reward was and still is a hard way to base one's life work.

Where Oke had concerned himself with building lighthouses on the major headlands, capes and prominent islands, Nevill began the second stage of lighthouse construction on the Island. He started to fill in the dark spaces between the original, primary lights. Most were built at the entrances to the major harbours located around the island. After completing Ferryland Head lighthouse, he built the lighthouse at the entrance to Trinity harbour on the site of an old English fort. Other lighthouses followed in quick succession: the Belleoram harbour lighthouse, the Boar Island lighthouse off Burgeo, the Long Point lighthouse above Twillingate, the Channel Head lighthouse at the entrance to Port aux Basques harbour, the lighthouse at Rocky Point at the entrance to Harbour Breton and the Point Verde lighthouse at the entrance to Placentia harbour. By 1880, Nevill had added fifteen more lighthouses to the system of lights around the Island, doubling the number that existed a decade before. He also developed a system of floating bouys devised to mark the dangerous reefs and shoals offshore.

This period of rapid expansion of the lighthouse system was helped along by the development of pre-cast iron towers. While this approach had been around since the 1840s, their use did not dominate the Service until the last quarter of the nineteenth century. This economical approach to lighthouse construction allowed Nevill to plan and budget for a lighthouse in one season, order and have it cast over the winter, and then have it erected and set into operation the following season. They hired one of Robert Oke's sons to do much of this work. Austin Oke had been taught well by his father, and became a master mechanic. Each summer he oversaw the construction of many of the new lighthouses and the installation of their complex light mechanisms. For a dozen years, he sailed from Long Point lighthouse at Twillingate on the northeast coast to Channel Head on the far side of the Island. Tragically he drowned in June 1887, while trying to land on Ireland Island at the head of LaPoille Bay on the south coast of Newfoundland. A new lighthouse had been built there the year before, and Oke had been sent to make adjustments to the light mechanism. The small boat that he was in upset and he was thrown into the icy water. Nevill wrote his death "deprived the lighthouses of the valuable services of one who had spent almost a lifetime among them and whose natural fitness made him most valuable." The accident highlights how those involved in the maintenance of those far-flung stations frequently had to risk their lives to carry out their duties.

In 1885, Nevill hired on a young clerk named Richard White. He was the son of Captain Edward White, a well-known sealing captain. Richard was at ease on the water for he had gone to sea with his father at an early age. Young and athletic, he travelled with John Nevill on his summer inspections. It was White who would be first over the side of the steamer for the long row to shore. His reputation as an athlete followed him through the rest of his life.

In March 1892, Nevill injured his ankle in a fall and was confined to his country house on Rae Island, part of what would eventually become Bowring Park. He must have watched in horror one summer afternoon that July, when most of St. John's went up in flames. His injury did not heal properly; he wrote in his 1893 Report, "It was deemed unadvisable that the inspection of the lighthouses should be performed by me, in consequence of weakness from my accident of last year still remaining, Mr. White was sent (instead)." Nevill never really recovered from the accident, and when his son Thomas died suddenly in 1895 leaving a wife and six children, Nevill retired.

Richard White began a third phase of lighthouse construction around the Island. In ten years he doubled the number of lighthouses from thirty-five in 1895 to seventy-two in 1905. Most of these were minor lights - small iron towers built at the entrances to the outport harbours. White also began the process of lighting the long indented coastline of Labrador. By 1910, he had built half a dozen lighthouses in places like Indian Tickle and Cut Throat Point and Double Point at Battle Harbour.

That year the Lighthouse Service was placed under control of the Minister of the Department of Marine and Fisheries. With over one hundred stations including lighthouses, fog alarms and leading lights to maintain, White's budget was almost $90,000. By the time he died in 1917, Inspector White had built another forty lighthouses, bringing the total to 132 stations. The cost of operating the Service was quickly increasing. They needed almost two hundred people - keepers and their assistants - to operate these lights. The requirement for supplying all the stations with the necessary kerosene for the lights, and food and heating coal for the keepers was threatening to overwhelm them.

In the spring of 1917, Richard White prepared his last report to the House of Assembly. In it, he described a new light mechanism that he had installed in four of his most recent lighthouses: "The illuminant used is Acetylene, the most luminiferous of all gases, the light energy of the Acetylene flame is many times greater than that of oil or petroleum flames, and when surrounded by a lens is more effective. Supplied with each of these lights is a most ingenious gas saving device called a Sun Valve, by means of which it is made possible to light and extinguish the flame without the aid of a keeper, thus doing away with his services." Richard White died six months later, but his ideas about the automation of the lighthouses would be heard again and again as the years went on.

The new Inspector, W. P. Rogerson, realized that the use of acetylene was really the only way they could get control of the growth of the Service's budget. It more than doubled in only three years, growing from about $120,000 in 1917 to $327,000 in 1920. By this point the Lighthouse Service had grown to consume more than fifty percent of the Department's budget. In 1921, Rogerson built eight new lighthouses, all using acetylene. That summer they built an acetylene gas plant on King's Wharf in St. John's. They had been sending empty canisters away to

New York to be refilled. Rogerson hoped that the plant, capable of generating enough gas for thirty lighthouses, would help to make the Colony self-sufficient.

They also began to consider the purchase of their own supply vessel. Previously the Lighthouse Service had chartered steamers each summer to supply the lighthouses. Rogerson wrote, "The Department was, this year, more seriously handicapped than ever because of not having at its disposal a small steamer for the above purpose. Coastal steamers and small craft are our only means of getting supplies to Stations all around our coast. The steamers cannot land supplies direct except in very few instances. The small schooners are not now procurable at any price when they are needed. Having in mind the fact that more than 150 Stations must be supplied, and that more than 200 Lights, Beacons, Fog Alarms and Buoys should be inspected, it must be obvious that this work has now reached dimensions where I am justified in earnestly recommending that, in the best interest of this service, in order that our lights and alarms may be kept running all the time and may be properly inspected, a suitable steamer be provided without delay for this work." They never did purchase the vessel because the financial picture for the Colony was growing worse.

Throughout the 1920s, the Lighthouse Service continued to add five or six new, small lighthouses each year, continuing the process of marking outport harbour entrances and dangerous islands offshore. Starting in 1921, the government of Prime Minister Richard Squires authorized the first in a series of loans to finance this work. As each year passed, the Department had to set aside more and more money to make interest payments on the loans. They were a symptom of the growing economic and financial difficulty facing the Newfoundland government. These problems began at the end of World War I. They borrowed nineteen million dollars to send the Royal Newfoundland Regiment overseas. By the end of the decade, the Newfoundland government was eighty million dollars in debt with sixty percent of its revenues going towards interest payments on their various loans.

On November 18, 1929, less than a month after the stock market crashed in New York, a devastating earthquake struck off the coast of the Burin Peninsula. The subsequent tidal wave killed twenty-seven people and caused over $500,000 damage. The following year, the world price for fish plummeted and the fishery failed. The World Depression struck hard in Newfoundland. Frederick Alderdice came into office after the debacle of the Richard Squires administration. Faced with quickly dwindling revenues, he realized that his government soon would default on their debt payments. The Canadian and British governments intervened and agreed to bail them out. They would cover two thirds of the accumulated debt, if Alderdice's government would allow a British

Commission to examine the financial problems facing them and comply with their recommendations. The *Amulree Report* was completed the next year. Repelled by the corruption and inefficiency of the earlier administrations, it recommended that Responsible government be suspended for a period of time and that Newfoundlands public affairs be dealt with by a Board of Commissioners. Alderdice really had no choice. In February, 1932, Newfoundland's financial responsibilities were transferred to the British government and the curious institution of *Commission of Government* came into being. The Commission consisted of three Newfoundland members and three British members. The existing Departments were combined into six portfolios. Each member of the Commission was responsible for a different portfolio. The Lighthouse Service was placed in the Department of Public Utilities. This arrangement remained throughout the 1930s and 1940s. It was the British government which maintained and operated the Newfoundland lighthouses. While another eighty minor lights were added, the lighthouse structures and light mechanisms never received the maintenance they needed and were allowed to slowly deteriorate.

After the War, the Newfoundland people were given the opportunity to decide what form of government they wanted. They had three choices: the continuation of the Commission of Government, a return to Responsible Government, or Confederation with Canada. After a divisive campaign and two referenda, Newfoundlanders voted narrowly to join Canada. Economic prudence supplanted their sense of nationhood. Britain's oldest Colony became Canada's tenth Province.

In the transfer of power, many of Newfoundland's responsibilities fell under the jurisdiction of Canadian government. The job of maintaining and operating her 237 lighthouses became the responsibility of the Department of Transportation in Ottawa. This Department had been created in November 1936, when the Federal Cabinet agreed to amalgamate all the transportation services under one Department. The new Department included the Air Services Branch, the Land Services Branch and the Marine Services Branch. It was this last Branch which was responsible for such diverse public policy areas as the Harbours Boards, ice-breaking services, the management of the St. Lawrence Seaway and the extensive canal systems of Central Canada. The Marine Services Branch also built and operated the Canadian system of navigational aids.

In March 1949, the Department of Transportation took over control of the Newfoundland lighthouses, taking with them about 300 lighthouse keepers and their assistants. They began at once to modernize and rehabilitate the existing system of lighthouses. Much of this work involved the replacement of the old acetylene mechanisms with electric lights. Most sites were still very inaccessible and required the use of

20

rather undependable diesel generators. In only a few years, the number of keepers was cut in half as the stations became electrified. Most of the keepers who stayed on were there just to make sure that those generators kept running. Their traditional role as keepers of the light had changed in only a decade. The new technology made them more caretakers than anything else; their biggest task was monitoring the operational status of the equipment. This role would quickly become redundant. As early as 1957, National Research Council of Canada began designing sun switches which could extinguish the electric lights during daylight hours.

The technology for navigation advanced quickly after the War. Electronic systems such as Decca, and later, Loran C meant that ships navigating in Newfoundland waters could locate themselves without the aid of the guiding light of the lighthouse. By the early 1970s, Marine Services Branch had developed electronic systems which could automate all equipment functions at the lighthouse. They developed an equipment monitoring system capable of tracking operations in remote locations. Video display equipment could scan a station to determine if unauthorized persons have entered the premises. There were systems which can determine if the main light had burned out, still other equipment could trigger a new bulb to rotate into position in minutes. They were freed from using diesel generators when they first developed disposable batteries and later arrays of solar panels.

Starting in the 1970s, the *Canadian Coast Guard*, as it was renamed, stepped up their program of lighthouse automation. In the past two decades, they successfully automated all but a few of the Newfoundland lighthouses. The program has been quite controversial for many. Fishermen, in particular, have objected to taking the keepers' out of the stations. They argued that an automatic light can't direct a Coast Guard cutter to a stricken inshore vessel. Given the caprices of Newfoundland weather, fishermen also appreciated the keepers ability to report local weather conditions whenever they needed it. The Coast Guard's policy was to maintain keepers at stations if they had an active role in Search and Rescue or special meterological work. Whether the changes made by the Coast Guard are wrong or right, most would agree that they have been doing an admirable job in facilitating the efficient movement of vessels in Newfoundland waters. For most mariners, words cannot express their thanks for the contribution the Canadian Coast Guard has made to marine safety offshore.

The Newfoundland system of lighthouses has been brought to the brink of the twenty-first century after an historic one hundred and eighty years of operation.

The Keepers and their Machines

"No circumstance whatever will excuse any keeper for failing to exhibit the lights in his charge at the prescribed time, or for neglecting to keep them burning with the greatest possible brilliancy."

from *Rules and Instructions for the Guidance of Light Keepers*, 1905

As our lives become more hectic and the noise of our twentieth century world rises to what seems like a din, some of us may be tempted to look back romantically to the days of the early lighthouse keepers. What a dream it would be - transported back a hundred years to a high cape on a faraway coast. Imagine a cool summer wind off the water, rippling the long green grass beneath a lighthouse tower. Its dazzling white profile stands out against a cobalt blue ocean that runs out to an azure sky. Gazing out into the bay, you make out a single sail. They are fishermen on their way to the fishing grounds. Their outport harbour, the nearest settlement, is miles away down the coast. The faint boom of sea swells crashing on the cliff below is broken by the cry of gulls circling. It is the only sound you hear. . . . . what a life the keeper must have had - a life of sweet peace and tranquillity . . . . . .

Unfortunately such an idyllic portrayal of a keeper's life couldn't be further from the truth. There may have been only a couple of days each summer when they could take the time to look up from their chores and gaze wistfully out to the horizon. The truth of the matter is their lives were bounded by a series of monotonous tasks, broken only by the passing of day and night. Beyond the tedium, their lives were imbrued with a pervasive sense of loneliness, for very few of the early stations were located near outport communities. This sense of loneliness was especially true for the wives of the keepers. They had not grown up on one of these isolated stations and many were quite unfamiliar with the life there. Their children often had to board at a distant town with relatives in order that they might be educated properly. The role of these women remained largely unrecorded. They frequently filled in for their husbands when they were sick or had to travel to St. John's. Ironically, there was never a case where a women held the formal responsibility of keeping a Newfoundland light. That job most often fell to the oldest son of the family. No matter who was ultimately responsible, the nineteenth century lighthouse keeper and his family had a hard, lonely life with too little in the way of support from the outside world.

The lives of the keeper and his family were set apart quite distinctively from those who lived in the outports. The people in the outports in the nineteenth century were synchronized with the seasons, their lives revolving around the inshore fishery. Throughout the year, fishermen would turn their small boats toward the fishing grounds while their wives and children worked at the fish flakes, salting and drying the cod. When they weren't fishing they had to tend their gardens and their animals, mend their nets or cut their winter wood. They made most of what they needed. Their salt cod was traded for the few necessities of life that they couldn't manufacture themselves. Molasses, tea, flour and sugar, twine for their nets and bolts of fabric for their clothing all came from the local merchant. While their salt water produce would fetch a princely sum in the European and American markets, they wouldn't see a penny of it. Theirs was a cashless society. The keepers, on the other hand, earned a salary from the Lighthouse Board. Take James Cantwell, for instance; he was the keeper at Cape Spear lighthouse in the 1850s and 1860s. He earned £100 sterling in 1866. While he still had to deal with the day to day drudgery of gardens, livestock and heating his house, the fact that he earned a salary and was part of the newly formed public service set him apart from his outport neighbours.

Early on, the Lighthouse Board both in Canada and in Newfoundland established a set of instructions to outline the duties of the keepers. Robert Oke mentioned them in his 1869 report: "The discipline and duties enjoined on the respective keepers, *by the printed instructions*, cannot be too stringently insisted upon, and with due zeal in the discharge of those duties, the several Light Houses cannot fail to retain that high character which has been awarded to them." The keepers were educated men in a rural society which still did not understand nor value education. In fact many keepers were so well read that they maintained a complete library in their offices. It would have contained a plethora of instructions on the operation of the light supplied by the Lighthouse Board. It would also contain various nautical charts and "how to" books on such diverse subjects as meteorology, medicine and animal husbandry. In their isolation, it could be months before St. John's would be able to respond if a problem occurred. The library also would have contained works of fiction by authors like Thoreau and Thackery, Chaucer and Shakespeare. These worn volumes were read and re-read during the long winter nights when the keepers were on duty in the tower.

"Unknow Keeper and his family."

The keepers also were expected to write effectively. They had to maintain daily logs indicating the amount of oil and other stores used. They also recorded daily weather and ice conditions and the passage of ships. If problems were encountered at the station, these would be described and their remedy communicated to head office in St. John's.

The keeper's logs formed the basis of the Inspector's report submitted to the House of Assembly each year.

Chances are the keeper had been the oldest son of the previous keeper. He had been trained by his father in the special skills of a keeper. The knowledge necessary to operate the light set them apart from the fishermen who lived nearby; this kind of technology was completely foreign to the outport people. The characteristic of having the keepership of a lighthouse remain in one family for generations was certainly true of Newfoundland's oldest lighthouses. The skills that they learned as children caused the Board to hire the next in a family when the elder keeper was ready to retire or passed away. All the Inspectors may not have agreed with this dynastic approach to keepership. John Nevill wrote in his 1880 report after a visit to England, "In the British lighthouse service, great care is exercised in the appointment of keepers..... The men are frequently removed from one station to another. This mobility has great advantages; it prevents local jealousies and favouritisms....It also prevents a keepership being regarded in an hereditary light, and such a system does away with the possibility of any station being officered by members of the same family."

The lives of everyone at the station - the keeper, his assistant and their families were dedicated to the maintenance of the light itself. While it was their *raison d'etre*, tending the light was a monotonous, time-consuming duty. Up to the late 1700s, only simple lamps were available as light sources. These lamps were unsuitable because they gave off large quantities of smoke - the result of imperfect combustion of the oil. The windows of the lighthouse would quickly become covered in layers of soot, dimming the brilliance of light. By the time the earliest lighthouses were built in Newfoundland, a new apparatus had been developed. It used a series of *Argand* lamps each set into a parabolic reflector. The system was described as *catoptric*, a term which came for the Greek meaning - *mirrored* or *reflected image*. The parabolic reflectors, unlike spherical reflectors, collected the rays of light and redirected them in a single concentrated beam. These reflectors could magnify the intensity of the light many times over.

In 1782, Ami Argand, an academic from Switzerland, developed a smokeless oil lamp that would later bear his name. The lamp was designed to allow more air to move over the hot portion of the flame. This allowed better combustion of the oil, gave a steadier flame and a more intense white light. Argand's lamp had two brass tubes or rings, one inside the other, with a hollow "sock-shaped" cotton wick held between them. With air passing on both sides of the lighted wick, the flame burned with less smoke. A circular, glass chimney controlled the air flow around the flaming wick and increased its brilliance even more.

Initially, the only oil suitable for the Argand lamps was the highly refined and expensive Sperm whale oil. As the use of these lamps became more common first in lighthouses, and later in commercial buildings and people's homes, demand for the oil increased. The whaling industry all around the world enjoyed a brief period of prosperity until the whale population began to decline under their pressure. In Newfoundland, the Lighthouse Board used Sperm oil in the first several years of their operation. But in 1841, the Board reconsidered its use.

> The Commissioners had long entertained the opinion that the best pale Seal Oil might be brought into use in the Light Houses in this Colony, but they were deterred from time to time from acting on this opinion from the fact of a quantity of Sperm Oil having been sent with the apparatus in the first instance as the only description that would be suitable..... But the expense under this head had now become intolerable, and the Commissioners determining no longer to regard the opinions by which they had hitherto been influenced, resolved to test the correctness of their own impression - that seal oil might be made to answer all their purposes. They accordingly tried the experiment by lighting two ordinary lamps, one with seal, and the other with sperm oil, and this proving satisfactory to their views, tenders were immediately advertised for a supply of pale seal oil for the consumption of the Light Houses for one year, which was furnished at a reasonable rate. The Commissioners immediately ordered that this oil should be used in the several establishments, and they are happy to state that the results have been fully such as they could have desired; an important saving is herby effected in the expenditure, being at a calculation of the cost of their last importation, not less than £400 sterling per annum.

All the early Newfoundland lighthouses used a catoptric mechanism. The light apparatus consisted of an array of eight to twelve Argand lamps and reflectors set in a metal frame. Every evening before dusk, the keeper had to light each of the lamps. Throughout the night, they were expected to make regular visits to the lantern room to make sure that the lamps were lit properly. This extra care was necessary because the variable winds outside affected the draft coming up the tower. Changes in the draft in turn varied the air flow over the wick causing the flame either to flare up or be blown out. While the keeper could adjust ventilating ports to control the draft somewhat, the lamps required constant attention. These ports, located around the perimeter of the lantern room, were installed to allow in fresh air. With so many lamps roaring away all night long, they could quickly consume all the oxygen in the room. A large ventilator was also placed in the apex of the roof to exhaust the considerable heat given off by the lamps.

There were many other duties associated with keeping the lamps shining brightly. During the night, if a lamp showed signs of diminution or dullness, the wick had to be trimmed, the chimney cleaned or changed and the draft adjusted. In foggy weather, the light had to operate on a twenty-four hour basis. In stormy weather, the light was even more carefully watched because the heavy gusts of wind could drastically alter the air flow over the flaming wick.

In the morning after the lights were extinguished, the silvered reflectors had to be gently polished with a dry chamois. The small tank for supplying the oil, attached to the back of each of the lamps, had to be filled by the keeper or his assistant. The illuminance of a catoptric apparatus depended on the number of lamps. The more lamps, the brighter its beam, but also the more oil consumed. In the 1860s, the lighthouse at Cape Bonavista with its sixteen Argand lamps used about 620 gallons of oil in a year. That worked out to about a gallon and a half of oil per day! The design of the early lighthouses provided for a large storage room directly beneath the lantern room, permitting easy access to the barrels of oil that were shipped out each summer by the Lighthouse Board.

Many of the lighthouses were built close enough to the shore to be drenched in storm-tossed sea spray. There would be many days in winter when the keeper and his family dared not set foot outside for fear of being blown away. The Lighthouse Board frequently built an enclosed walkway leading from the residence to the lighthouse tower for this reason. The large panes of glass in the lantern room quickly became encrusted with dried salt. The panels had to be washed periodically to avoid the diminution of the light. If they were lucky, the keeper could use an iron catwalk that was built around the perimeter of the lantern room for that purpose. A bosun's chair slung on a block and tackle was their only other alternative.

The primary purpose of the lighthouses was to help navigators fix their position as they travelled along the coast. This was especially true in the case of the *landfall* lights that a mariner first sighted on approaching land. As more and more lights were built, they had an increasingly difficult time distinguishing one fixed light from another fixed light. Ideally, the landfall lighthouses would have a unique characteristic which would allow easy recognition by those on board a wayward ship. In the late eighteenth century a Swede by the name of Jonal Norberg developed the idea of rotating the whole light apparatus on its axis. From a distance, the revolving light would appear to flash rather than show a fixed light. Using a simple mechanical system, the keeper could regulate the rate of the revolutions effectively controlling the period between each flash. A flashing light would certainly catch a mariner's attention and its individual characteristics would clearly identify it. By the 1860s at least half the lighthouses built by Robert Oke used revolving mechanisms. Since then many of our important lights have used this same idea.

While use of revolving lights proved successful, its mechanical solution added to the keeper's daily chores. The light mechanism with its array of lamps and reflectors was supported on a circular, cast iron vessel which floated in a corresponding circular trough filled with mercury. The heavy liquid was used as a bearing for the apparatus, allowing it to rotate with minimum friction. The mercury could also absorb much of the vibration and movement in the tower, reducing damage to the sensitive apparatus. The keepers were expected to drain the trough of its mercury periodically and attempt to remove dust, dirt and metal filings that built up there. There are stories of several Canadian keepers slowly going insane from their improper handling of the deadly mercury.

The light apparatus revolved by means of a spring-operated clock mechanism. It worked much like a cuckoo clock, driven by a heavy weight fixed to the end of a chain. The weight would slowly sink down the full height of the lighthouse through a *weight tube*. The trip down would take two to three hours depending on the height of the tower. A bell or gong warned the keeper that it was time to wind the weight back up to the top of the tower again. This task had to be repeated a number of times each night. If one of the springs broke, the keeper, his assistant and their families all pitched in to rotate the apparatus by hand until the necessary parts could be replaced.

It had been known for centuries that a curved piece of glass could be used to concentrate the rays of the sun. How often have we as children, used a magnifying glass on a sunny day to burn a hole in a piece of paper. In the 1820s, a Swiss scientist, Augustin Fresnel, built a cage-like apparatus made of rings of glass arranged one above the other in an oval metal frame. It looked like an enormous, beautifully intricate glass beehive. These rings were actually glass lenses placed so they could collect all the rays of a light positioned in the centre and concentrate them into a powerful horizontal beam of light. The main rays passed through a central band of lenses known as the *bull's eye*. While the single lamp remained still, the glass cage was designed to revolve in a mercury trough. This apparatus was known as a *dioptric* light, referring to the way the light was refracted or bent by the glass lenses.

The system would revolutionize the way lighthouses worked, for it could increase the power of the light several hundred thousand times. Its most immediate benefit was that it needed only a single lamp, saving huge quantities of oil. Ideally, this lamp had to give off as much light as possible. Chance Brother Limited, the famous English manufacturers of lighthouse optics, perfected huge lamps that consisted of a series of concentric wicks, one inside the other. The wicks in some of these lamps were as wide as ten centimetres across. Lit together, they could exhibit an extraordinarily large flame. Their large size made them difficult to light. The keepers had to remain by the lamp for nearly an hour, slowly increasing the flow of oil, until the burner was hot enough to combust the oil properly.

The keeper was expected to carefully clean each glass prism and lens every day. After the cleaning, a white flannel shroud was placed over the apparatus to protect it until the evening. Given the size of many of these dioptric mechanisms, this cleaning posed quite a task. The larger mechanisms contained as many as fifteen glass rings, each eighteen inches in diameter. The dioptric light placed in the new lighthouse at Cape Race in 1907 was one of the largest ever built. It was eight feet in diameter and weighed seven tons. Imagine cleaning that monster every morning!

"Cape Race Light Mechanism, 1907."

The Newfoundland keepers had to deal with the problem of running out of the paraphernalia necessary to exhibit the light properly. The tall, thin-walled glass chimneys were easy to break, and the variously sized wicks burnt away quickly. Many of the lamp's bits and pieces had to be replaced on a monthly basis. While the Lighthouse Board strove to get needed supplies to the isolated stations, the amazingly rugged topography often prevented the supplies from getting through. Inspector Nevill expressed his frustration in his 1872 Report. "Many Light House Keepers complain of not receiving the stores shipped to them, this has been the case for many years past. That arises from the hurry and confusion of landing at difficult and dangerous places, the natural desire of the master of the contract vessel to get clear of such as quickly as possible, and from no person other than the master being present to see the work performed accurately. I should recommend that in future a reliable supercargo be sent.... to see the stores properly landed at their respective destinations." Nevill's term *supercargo* was the name given to an officer on board a merchant ship whose business it was to ensure that the cargo got to its proper destination.

On a clear night, how far out to sea that a light could be seen was limited by the curvature of the earth. Many of the lighthouses, particularly on the east and northeast coasts were built atop the highest cliff that they could find. Often a suitable landing area could not be found within miles. The prospect of carting the four or five hundred gallons of oil up over the highlands was a daunting task. In several cases there simply wasn't a place to land; they were forced to use a large wooden boom for the transfer. They would unload the supplies from the chartered steamer into a small boat. The crates and barrels were then ferried to a point just beneath the sheer cliff face. A line was lowered and the load hoisted, piece by piece, up to the keeper waiting at the top of the cliff. This job was quite hazardous and couldn't be attempted unless the conditions were very calm. It often meant that the supplies were damaged or didn't get through at all.

"Boom and tackle for hoisting supplies; Marticot Island."

courtesy of Transport Canada

During these summer visits, the Lighthouse Service supplied all the food and heating coal needed by the keeper for the entire year. The stations frequently ran out of these essentials and the keepers and their families suffered greatly. What food they received was often damaged or rotten by the time they finally could open up the crates. The obvious solution to this problem was to grow their own food or to try to hunt it on the barrens or catch it in the nearby ocean. If there was sufficient soil, the keepers and their families became quite adept at growing large gardens and maintaining flocks of chickens, sheep, goats and pigs. Most keepers had large families; all were enlisted to help out in those household chores. Unfortunately, the soil on these treeless capes and headlands was at a premium.

The isolation posed another deadly problem. If a member of the family became ill, they had to know what to do or go untreated until the unlucky soul either died or grew better on his/her own. Firewood was scarce. If their meagre supplies of heating coal ran out, conditions in their living quarters could grow very cold and damp. They often suffered from frequent bouts of pneumonia, tuberculosis and arthritis. There were also cases of diphtheria, cholera and typhoid in the Newfoundland lighthouse stations. These deadly diseases could wipe out entire families at a time. Unsanitary conditions and contaminated water breed bacteria responsible for these highly infectious diseases. They were swift killers. Families would rarely have time to summon a doctor from a distant outport before the hapless victim succumbed. The Lighthouse Board included a detailed set of instructions on how to treat most of the common illnesses, but without the proper medicines, they weren't much use. The instructions recommended simple organic mixtures designed to reduce some of the symptoms of the diseases. It would not be until the next century and the development of powerful antibiotics that they would finally be able to cope with illness at the stations.

The lighthouse technology continued to improve as the nineteenth century progressed, easing some of the strain in the system. In 1846, a Nova Scotian inventor named Abraham Gesner developed a new illuminant which would be used in Newfoundland lighthouses for nearly fifty years. He distilled oil from coal and called it *kerosene* or mineral oil. When vaporized, it would burn more cleanly and brightly than seal oil. Smaller quantities could produce greater candle power. It was first used in Newfoundland in 1873 on Cann Island off Fogo Island and Boar Island off Burgeo.

Chance Brothers perfected an Incandescent oil vapour lamp in the 1870's using kerosene. The design of the lamp was similar to the present day "Coleman" lantern used by campers. Compressed-air forced kerosene into a vaporizing chamber. The hot walls of the chamber turned the liquid oil into a gas. The oil vapour would then pass up into a mantle where it was consumed in a glowing, bright gas ball. With each new improvement in the lamps, the illuminance increased and the amount of fuel required declined. Unfortunately, these oil vapour lamps were just as difficult to maintain as the previous Argand lamps. The Newfoundland Lighthouse Service began to convert to lamps using acetylene in the 1920s. Acetylene burned very brightly and did not require the same amount of cleaning as the earlier fuels. For the first time, the idea of automatic stations became a possibility. Each evening, a sun switch could trigger a pilot light to ignite the lamps.

Parallel to the developments of light mechanisms was the development of fog alarms. Newfoundland was and still is famous for its sea fogs. These dense fogs are formed when warm winds off the land blow over much colder sea water. The icy Arctic Current passes southward along the northeastern and eastern coasts of the Island from the Davis Sea off Baffin Island. The waters off the east coast of Newfoundland are known to be some of the foggiest in the world. The situation is particularly bad in the late spring and early summer. July is usually the worst month; the coasts can be foggy for fifty percent of the time.

When these dripping fogs set into a coastline, even the most powerful lighthouses were ineffective, their light only penetrating a hundred metres at most. A sound signal rather than a light signal was needed here. The Fort Amherst lighthouse used a cannon to mark the entrance to St. John's harbour. Operated by a small contingent of British Artillery men, it fired once every hour in foggy conditions. The practice of firing an explosive charge at this lighthouse continued until the 1911. The lighthouse at Point Amour on the south coast of Labrador also used a *dynamite gun* as it was known. An assortment of bells, gongs and sirens were tried in Britain, Canada and the United States as alternatives to the cannon.

In 1858, Robert Foulis, a Canadian inventor from Saint John, New Brunswick developed the first steam-driven fog whistle. In the decades that followed, steam whistle fog alarms were built at many of the major lighthouse stations around the Island. Cape Race, Cape St. Francis, Cape Spear, Cape Ray and Cape Norman all saw the construction of these types of fog alarms. Powered by a large boiler, the equipment needed a ready supply of water. At times, this posed quite a problem on the rocky capes. The steam engine also required huge quantities of coal. This caused many problems of supply in the last half of the nineteenth century. The fog alarms would add a new dimension to the life at the stations. The boiler's voracious appetite for coal meant that more men had to be located at the stations. Inspector Nevill had to frequently deal with the problem of coal consumption. He reported that in August of 1882, the Cape Race fog alarm operated for a total of 380 hours. It obviously had been a particularly bad month for fog. The engineers shovelled twenty-six tons of coal into the gaping mouth of the boiler. That's nearly two tons of coal a day, quite a bit of shovelling for anyone.

The machinery was slowly refined with time to require less water and less coal. But it seems that they could not overcome another problem associated with the steam whistles. At sea, a steam whistle could easily be mistaken for a ship's whistle. The effectiveness of a fog alarm depended in part upon its ability to carry across the water. It also needed a characteristic sound which made it instantly recognizable, its meaning not confused by other similar sounds.

In 1902, the Toronto manufacturer, J.P. Northery Limited, developed a fog alarm that would become famous around the world. They called the new fog alarm a *Diaphone*. While the diaphones used com-

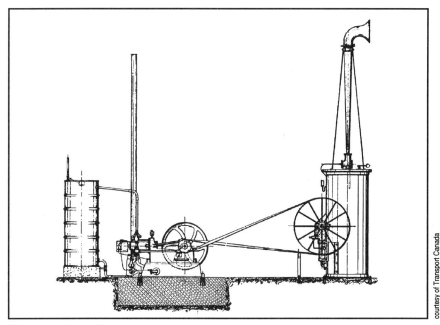

Diaphone from 1910

pressed air, they required much less power compared to the previous steam whistles and sirens. More importantly, it produced a very distinctive, tremendously loud sound with its characteristic "grunt" at the end of each blast. It was said that mariners could hear the diaphone's steady warning at ranges exceeding twenty miles out to sea. The design also allowed for precise control of the blast interval and was easy to maintain compared to the earlier systems. Before long, many of the old steam alarms in Newfoundland were replaced by diaphones. After World War II, new fog alarms similar to the diaphone operating with electric air compressors were developed.

The coming of electricity spelled the end of the life of the lighthouse keeper as it was known in the nineteenth century. Their role changed to one of a caretaker. The light exhibited in the filament in an electric bulb meant that there was no flame, no soot, and no need for the daily cleaning of the lenses and the constant attention to the lamps. Electric timers and light sensors could automatically turn on the light apparatus at dusk and turn off again at sunrise.

At the few stations that retained a keeper, a modern, well insulated bungalow was built, drawing power from a diesel generator. Electric heating, a deep freezer filled with groceries and a satellite dish meant that they would have all the comforts of home. If something happened while they were on station, an injured keeper was only hours away from twentieth century health services. Today, a team of two or more keepers spell each other on alternating shifts. This allows them to have a normal life in town with their families when they are not at the station. In the very near future, computer technology and satellite communications will allow all the keepers to be withdrawn.

Looking back on one hundred and fifty years of responsibility, it seems the lighthouse keepers have earned an honoured spot in the minds of mariners and fishermen who have sailed along the Newfoundland coasts. While the Lighthouse Board did have the occasional problem with discipline, the keepers as a group were devoted to the duty. Most keepers did what they felt that their job called for, even when their own lives were at risk. Most of these men wouldn't think twice to attempt to rescue survivors of a shipwreck at the edge of a sea-washed cliff or remain in the lantern room keeping the lamps going long after they should have retreated in the face of a hurricane. Some of these stories of their bravery are retold in the chapters that follow. Most of these men wouldn't understand the attention paid to them here for it was only in a day's work.

Fort Amherst
(Flash 7 seconds; eclipse 3 seconds)
The Harbour Light

"When you get Two Leagues at Sea the Settlement of St. John's has a very pretty effect. The White Fort on the left, Signal Hill on the right, the high Cliffs on each side which forms the Narrows and the distant Hills produce a pleasing Landscape. The Harbour's mouth, called the Narrows, is defended by Fort Amherst and Two other Batteries."
from *the Journal of Aaron Thomas*, 1794

Imagine the amazement of the early European fishermen when they first passed through the narrow channel that separates the North Atlantic from the harbour at St. John's. The coastline that runs along the eastern edge of the Avalon Peninsula rises to form a high, dangerous rock barrier to the North Atlantic. This coastline affords very few sheltered harbours for those travelling along its shore. The landlocked shape of St. John's harbour was the perfect haven for those sea-weary visitors. The early fishermen realized that it was capable of holding hundreds of sailing ships.

No one is really sure when European fishermen first discovered this outstanding harbour. Historians feel that it could have taken place in the final years of the fifteenth century. Accounts of John Cabot's first visit describe "this year on St. John the Baptist day (June 24, 1497), the land . . . .. was found by the merchants of Bristol." Cabot later named the place *St. John's Island* after the Saint on whose feast day it was first sighted.

Another explorer, John Rut, who followed Cabot thirty years later, found St. John's harbour occupied by an assortment of fishermen and merchantmen from all over Europe. Rut wrote a letter to his sponsor King Henry VII from St. John's harbour. He recommended that the hearty West Country merchants be encouraged to settle in the wonderful place. He described it as "the" haven of St. John's Island. This recognition of the excellent harbour might help explain the curious name - St. John's.

In the centuries that followed, St. John's would become a sort of "way station" for the various explorers and colonists bound for North America. The harbour was located midway between Cape Bonavista and Cape Race, along what would eventually be known as the "English Shore." It was located next to one of the best fishing grounds in the world. St. John's harbour would become well known to the Basque, the French, the Portuguese and the English, as they travelled each spring from their home ports to establish summer fishing stations there.

Jacques Cartier visited St. John's in 1542, after one of his historic journeys to the New World. He found his Sieur Jean de la Roche, Seigneur de Roberval there with three ships full of colonists bound for Montreal. Other explorers including Henry Hudson and Samuel Champlain passed through the narrow harbour entrance on their way to greater glory on the mainland.

The strategic importance of St. John's harbour was not overlooked by the maritime nations of Europe. Queen Elizabeth I sent Sir Humphrey Gilbert to claim Newfoundland for England in 1583. When Gilbert arrived in August of that year, he found the harbour full of foreign vessels. It took a bit of persuading before Gilbert could enter the harbour and complete his mission.

Not surprisingly, this English claim was not respected by the other European nations. During the Second Dutch War against the English in the summer of 1665, Admiral Michiel de Rutyer led a fleet of warships through the Narrows at St. John's. He was the Commander-in-chief of the Royal Dutch Navy. That year, he sacked and burned the fishing station to the ground. He became famous a few years later, when he took his warships up the Thames to make a daring attack on the outskirts of London. Admiral de Rutyer made another attempt to destroy the settlement in 1674 but an English merchant named Christopher Martin mounted several cannons at the entrance of the harbour and drove de Rutyer's fleet off. For the little English outpost in Newfoundland, de Rutyer's attacks began almost one hundred and fifty years of armed conflict.

It was around the same time that the French had established a garrison fort at Placentia on the southeast coast of Newfoundland. In the decade that followed, petitions were made to the British Admiralty by the merchants using St. John's harbour. They felt that fortifications were necessary to protect their lucrative fishing businesses from interference by the French. The first modest fortification was built by the English after the last Dutch attack. This early fort, later known as the "Southside Castle", was built on a grassy knoll that rises on the southern side of the Narrows at the foot of the Southside Hills. A well-built, five-foot-thick, stone wall was constructed to withstand cannon fire from hostile ships attempting to enter the harbour. The masonry wall rose 12 feet from the level of the beach and ran 100 feet down the rocky shore. The wall was divided up into sixteen-foot compartments probably designed to accommodate heavy cannons mounted above. A wooden palisade was constructed to protect the landward approaches to the coastal fort. Ten years later, a second major fortification was built at the bottom of Signal Hill commanding the north side of the harbour entrance. It was known as Fort William. Today, Hotel Newfoundland is built on this site.

These two forts were put to their first test in the summer of 1696. Chevalier Nesmond led a squadron of frigates from Placentia to attempt to force their way into the harbour at St. John's. English fishermen and merchants who were occupying the harbour that season manned the two forts and established a wicked cross-fire. They managed to drive the French warships from the Narrows.

Later in the fall of the same year, Pierre Le Moyne, Sieur d'Iberville, made plans to attack St. John's from Placentia. He was under orders from his commander, Louis, Buade de Frontenac at Quebec City to make another attempt at destroying the English settlement. The French chose not to make a frontal attack through the Narrows. In November 1696, d'Iberville took a strong force of four hundred French marines and Micmacs overland across the southern Avalon Peninsula to attack Ferryland. They went on to burn Bay Bulls and Petty Harbour. They hiked from there up over the highlands and entered St. John's from the west, marching down the Waterford Valley. The few inhabitants who had remained at the outpost that fall put up a heroic fight. After a bloody two-day battle, the experienced French troops took the station and burnt it to the ground.

The next spring, 1500 English troops arrived and found the station abandoned. That year, they established the first garrison at St. John's and promptly set about rebuilding the town's defence. Captain Michael Richards, a Royal Engineer, rebuilt the Castle on the Southside, mounting "six great guns" on its rampart. He had a heavy chain boom stretched across the two-hundred-foot Narrows to a large rock projecting from the water's edge on the north side. This rock became known appropriately enough as "Chain Rock." The chain was intended to prevent enemy ships from entering the harbour. It was a technique that would be used in every war that was to follow. In World War II, steel nets were employed to prevent German submarines from entering the harbour.

It was during this time that Captain Richards also fortified the southern side of the entrance to the Narrows. Richards wanted to build a battery that would be a first defence against an attack by sea. This site would house the first Newfoundland lighthouse a century later. The fort began as a simple wooden platform built to house a series of mortars or light cannon.

In 1702, the Queen Ann's War broke out between England and France. Again, the rich fishery and strategic location drew the attention of both countries to Newfoundland. By the winter of 1705, another strong force of four hundred French volunteers and regulars attempted to replicate d'Iberville's successful attack. They were led by Monsieur de Subercasse, the Governor of Placentia. Subercasse landed at Bay Bulls and Petty Harbour and marched on St. John's. They managed to take much of the civilian town, leaving only the Southside Castle and Fort William. The Castle was manned by a small band of militia and townsfolk. Using block and tackle, the French hoisted four cannons up on the heights above the fort and "formed a guard to harass them day and night." The inhabitants of the Castle must have been a resolute lot for they resisted the siege for over a month. Eventually the French, enveloped in a miserable Newfoundland winter, and low on food and ammunition, returned to Placentia without taking the forts.

It was four years to the month when the French attacked again; this time they used stealth rather than brute force to succeed. During the night of December 21, 1708, one hundred and sixty-four men crept into the settlement, evading the sentries to penetrate Fort William. They took it in thirty minutes after a bloody fight. The Castle surrendered the next day. By late March, the French had withdrawn, but not before they levelled the Southside Castle, demolishing probably the oldest British fortification in North America.

The War did not go well for the French on the continent. In the peace treaty signed in the Dutch city of Utrecht in 1713, they were forced to abandon all claims to Newfoundland. They fled from their stronghold in Placentia to Cape Breton, building a powerful fortress at Louisbourg, and settled on the fertile shores of Ingonish.

In the War of Austrian Succession that followed, Colonel Wolfe defeated Montcalm on the Plains of Abraham near Quebec City. Faced with imminent defeat in North America, the French government decided that they should capture an English possession to use as a bargaining chip during negotiations for peace. By then Halifax had been heavily fortified so they prepared to make the fifth attack on the fishing station at St. John's.

In the spring of 1762, four warships left Brest with seven hundred marines bound for the eastern coast of Newfoundland. This armed force was lead by Count D'Haussonville. They landed at Bay Bulls and marched on St. John's. Confronted with an overwhelming superiority of troops, the English garrison at St. John's capitulated on June 27. When word reached the New England colonies, a contingent of the Royal American Regiment was readied in an attempt to wrestle the fishing outpost back from the French invaders. Lieutenant Colonel William Amherst landed north of St. John's at Torbay with seven hundred crack troops and marched on St. John's. After a pitched battle at the King's Bridge, the English forced their way around the lake to the outport at Quidi Vidi Gut. It was through this tiny harbour that Amherst was able to land enough troops and artillery to press his attack up Signal Hill that evening. He took the top of the hill and turned the guns down on to the French-held Fort William. Count D'Haussonville realized that they would soon be cut off from the sea by an English squadron lying off the coast. They promptly loaded up their four frigates and slipped one by one out through the harbour entrance in the night.

The Treaty of Paris was signed the next year. The French dropped all claim to their North American possessions. The tiny islands of Saint Pierre and Miquelon off the south coast of Newfoundland were ceded to France; the islands are still a French Protectorate even today.

It seems that the British learned their lesson after this last episode with D'Haussonville. In 1762, they began a fortification program in St. John's that began at the rocky entrance to the harbour. It was William Amherst who realized the importance of establishing a strong outpost at the outer reaches of the harbour. It was from this point that they could easily command those ships who entered and left the harbour. He named it Fort Amherst not after himself but after his brother Jeffrey who led the English troops to victory at Louisbourg four years before. Plans for the fort were prepared in 1763 by a Royal Engineer named Pringle. It was not completed until 1777. It is said to have consisted of a white-washed stone battery with a wooden platform behind. The battery was built to hold as many as seventeen cannons, most of them the large twenty-four pound variety. This complex also contained a barracks, a mess hall and several buildings for the men stationed there. In those days, this rocky point was inaccessible by land. It could be reached only by crossing over a rickety system of wooden bridges and boardwalks around the base of the Southside Hills.

Paul O'Neil, in his book *St. John's: A Seaport Legacy*, describes many tragic and sometimes humurous incidents which took place at the entrance to St. John's harbour. He tells the story of military security that enveloped the Town in the years after Fort Amherst was completed. The military governors began a practice known as "Let-Pass." The Let-Pass was a paper prepared by the administration which indicated that the ships and their owners sailing out of harbour, were up to date on their port duties and taxes. The completed form had to be received by the commanding officer at Fort Amherst before the ship would be allowed to pass through the Narrows. Without it, the captain risked getting a broadside from the twenty-four pounders trained on the entrance. This rather mean approach to port-administration ended nearly fifty years later. An over-zealous gunner found himself in court after nearly taking the stern off a local merchantman that was attempting to escape from the harbour without paying his port dues.

In the late eighteenth century to the end of the War of 1812, the port of St. John's remained very much a strongly held provisioning point for the British Navy. There was considerable traffic during these years as warships travelled on their way to and from the North American colonies. In the spring of 1788, the infamous Captain William Bligh on board HMS *Bounty* passed by Fort Amherst for a brief visit to St. John's. He was on his way to Tahiti to collect breadfruit to feed the slaves of Jamaica.

After the chaos of the French Revolution, with the rise in power of Napoleon, another long war broke out between a French/Spanish coalition and the English. It would last for twenty years. With the powerful English fleet, a naval blockade of French and Spanish ports began. In 1797, Admiral Richery, intent on harassing and destroying as much English shipping and property as possible, managed to slip through the blockade at Cadiz in Spain. It was said that he had a powerful fleet with three heavily armed Ships of the Line. These were enormous ships, over two hundred feet in length, with a crew of 850 men carrying as many as ninety 18-pounder-cannons on three decks. His squadron also included four double-decked frigates each having 74 guns apiece together with another four sloops carrying another 24 guns apiece.

Richery made for St. John's, figuring that with his superior fire power, he could pound Fort Amherst into submission. With the battery silenced, he could then force his way into the harbour to destroy the town.

The steel nerves and the ingenuity of Governor John Wallace proved to be more than a match for Admiral Richery. It was the morning of September 2, 1796, when the French fleet was sighted off the coast. Unfortunately, Wallace did not have a large garrison in St. John's at the time. He developed a plan to fool the French into thinking that St. John's would be too costly to try to take. He had his men erect tents on both sides of the entrance to the Narrows and then marched them to and fro at Fort Amherst and below Signal Hill.

Richery's huge fleet had been hove to off Cape Spear for the day observing the daunting sight. The next morning, he formed a battle line and drove for the harbour entrance. As they came within the range of those twenty-four pounders at Fort Amherst, his resolve weakened. Tacking the great ships, he headed back out to sea. The ruse had worked - the old garrison town was saved. Richery went on to attack and burn the smaller settlements at Bay Bulls, Cape Broyle, Ferryland and the English garrison at Placentia.

Drawn by Pocock, engraved by Baily for the *The Naval Chronicle*, London, 1811.

"Entrance to St. John's Harbour, 1811."

The following year, Admirals Nelson and Jervis almost destroyed the Spanish fleet at Cape St. Vincent. At Trafalgar in 1805, Nelson finished the job. A final lasting peace was declared between England and France after the Battle of Waterloo in 1815.

This peace was much to the relief of the fishermen and West Country merchants stationed in St. John's. By then, the very successful fishery was attracting a considerable influx of English and Irish immigrants to the naval outpost. The population in the town doubled in the first ten years after the turn of the century. In 1810, Governor Duckworth yielded to the public's wishes and granted permission to build the first permanent houses in St. John's. The British Newfoundland Squadron was stationed in St. John's. It consisted of three magnificent Ships of the Line and twenty-one frigates. It was from St. John's that this powerful squadron raided the eastern seaboard of the United States during the War of 1812. Many an American prize was towed past Fort Amherst, on her way into St. John's harbour.

The prevailing wind at St. John's was ideal for ships entering the harbour. Under normal conditions a sailing vessel could easily pass through the one-half mile channel to the safety of the inner harbour. In a severe winter storm with a heavy sea pounding the sheer red sandstone cliffs, it was a different matter. The prospect of entering the one-thousand-foot-wide entrance should be better described as threading the eye of a needle. In the frequent dense fogs, mariners had to be right on the entrance before they could even detect it. After the War of 1812, there was an increase in the sea activities related to the booming fishery around St. John's. Also, there was an increase in the number of merchant ships supplying the young and growing colony. As a consequence of these two factors, the number of shipwrecks around the entrance to the harbour began to rise dramatically.

On the morning of December 4, 1811, a large "Western" schooner, the *Paradise*, loaded with fish and oil was attempting to enter the Narrows. She struck the vertical cliffs of North Head right across from Fort Amherst. The *Paradise* immediately went to pieces; five passengers died including two women, two men and a young girl. Just twelve days later another schooner the *Betsy*, loaded with coal and other provisions out of Sydney, Nova Scotia struck the jagged rocks at South Head just below the Fort. She also sank instantly. The Captain and one of the crew didn't make it out of the frigid water.

The next summer, Governor Duckworth, in response to the public outcry, established a pilotage service designed to help vessels into and out of the harbour. "Those who refused the use of a pilot did so at their own peril," the good Governor said. He may have been mistaken in his advice, at least in those early days. A month after he had issued his decree, a large schooner named the *Vulture* owned by a Guernsey merchant was lost at the harbour entrance while under a pilot's control. In a report to the owner, which followed after the wreck, they explained:

> "I acquaint you with the loss of your schooner *Vulture* . . .. in consequence of the pilot's imprudence in attempting to bear through the Narrows into this harbour. In going about, he went to the south side and in consequence thereof lodged upon a rock . . .. The Guernsey captain is now in this port and about 120 men from HMS *Antelope* succeeding in saving the cargo, and in 30 days and not 'til then, in getting the mast and rigging ashore."

The consensus of the fishing and commercial interests in St. John's was that a beacon or light should be built to mark the entrance to the Narrows at South Head. It was built in the stone tower erected inside the fort. The light was a simple mechanism consisting of three reflectors, illuminated with whale oil lamps. The light was maintained by the garrison in the Fort from voluntary contributions made by the merchant houses using the harbour between 1813 to 1835.

When Governor Cochrane established the Colonial Legislature in 1835, Fort Amherst lighthouse came under the control of the newly appointed Commissioners of Lighthouses. Philip Roach was appointed as the first civilian lighthouse keeper at Fort Amherst.

In their first report to the House of Assembly, the Commissioners complained: " ...It is, however, the contemplation of the Commissioners to procure a more effective Harbour Light as early as possible, the cost of which, the Commissioners are informed will amount to about £70...." It is unfortunate that the administration did not act on their recommendation at that time. The replacement, when it finally came, cost many times more than their original estimate. The Colonial government was intent on a building program to light the major headlands on the east coast of Newfoundland. This first lighthouse at Fort Amherst continued to deteriorate.

In the evening of February 1, 1848, after a long voyage from Scotland with a load of coal, the brigantine *Avalon* neared the entrance to St. John's harbour. The sea was full of pack ice, blocking the Narrows, so the *Avalon* anchored below Fort Amherst to wait for a shift in the wind. A terrific gale developed that night, and the *Avalon* began to drag her anchors into the cliffs below the fort. She was smashed in minutes. Those onshore rescued five crew members. The remaining five clung to the rigging until they finally succumbed to the freezing sea.

The following year, Patrick Kough, one of the Lighthouse Commissioners, indicated: "The lantern here is quite a flimsy concern, it was constructed about thirty years ago, and now so infirmed and decayed, as that if touched at all, it must be renewed." The administration relented and approved the replacement of the lighthouse in 1850.

They required special permission from the British government, because the old fort was still considered an active military installation. The influence by the military continued on to the design of the new lighthouse that was built in 1852. The main portion of the building was a 35' by 20', two-storey structure built to house a garrison of five soldiers. Their sole purpose was to keep a watchful eye on passing ships and to discharge a heavy cannon during the frequent periods of fog that obscured the harbour entrance. The four-foot stone walls were whitewashed and the slate roof was painted red to make it more distinctive.

A 12' by 15' extension was centered at the rear of the main building, so that it formed the letter "T" in plan. It was here that the lighthouse keeper and his family were to live. Philip Roach died during the construction of the new lighthouse. John Sheppard moved in to the keeper's quarters when the building was completed.

A short tower rose at the apex of the structure. New triple Argand lamps were installed there. Illuminated by seal oil, the mechanism cast a fixed white light. On a clear day, it could be seen twelve miles out to sea. The cost to build the new lighthouse complete with it's mechanism was over £1000 sterling. The new mechanism required constant tinker-

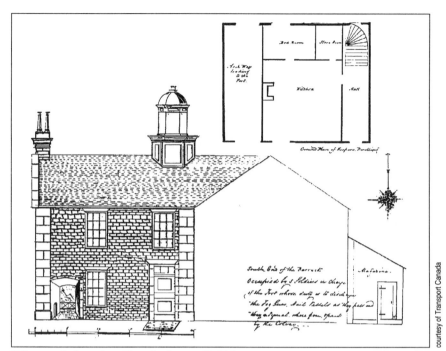

"Plan and elavation, Fort Amherst, 1860."

ing to maintain it in good working order. A local mechanic named William Molloy was employed during those years for that purpose. He was related to James Cantwell, the keeper at Cape Spear, and it is thought that this is how he got the job.

Another tragedy took place at Fort Amherst in 1876. The brigantine *Julia* was departing St. John's in the evening of October 15 of that year. She was loaded with salt cod headed for the Mediterranean. At 11 pm, her bottom was ripped open as she passed too close to the jagged rocks below the lighthouse. Sheppard and his family listened in horror as the sinking ship dragged thirteen souls down to the bottom of the Narrows.

In January 1887, Austin Sheppard took over from his father who was retiring because of ill health. The mid 1880s had seen other changes to the southern side of the "Narrows." John Wareham settled in the cove just west of Fort Amherst to pursue the fishery in the waters outside the harbour. His ancestors live there today in homes at the end of the drive that skirts Southside Hill. They watched in terror on a hot July day in 1892 when nearly the entire town went up in a huge conflagration. Austin Sheppard had rowed his new wooden skiff to Queen's Wharf that morning. Sheppard managed to escape with his life, but the new boat was burned to the waterline along with the whole wharf.

The small armed garrison remained at Fort Amherst during these years. They manned what was known locally as *the Dynamite Gun*. The

"Fort Amherst and North Head."

soldiers would fire a three pound charge from a single cannon on the stroke of every hour and when the harbour entrance was enshrouded in fog. Inspector Nevill reported that the cannon was fired 961 times in 1888! The vibrations from the big 32 pounder caused the stone lighthouse to be damaged and require constant repair. These problems were aggravated by the penetration of salt spray into the mortar joints. In

"Fog gun at Fort Amherst."

1893, the storm-swept wall on the northeastern side of the lighthouse finally failed and had to be replaced.

Problems with the structure continued. After ten years of constant repair, the old cannon was replaced by a system that used cartridges of gun cotton. The charge was hoisted up a high steel arm and fired electrically. This system was much less expensive, allowing them to fire the charge once every 20 minutes during foggy conditions. They moved the mechanism to the very western edge of the fort in an attempt to reduce some of the vibration. In 1911, a new diaphone finally silenced the old "dynamite gun" forever.

If Austin Sheppard had been on duty on the evening of October 14, 1909, he would have witnessed one of the most unusual incidents ever to take place in the harbour. The schooner *Veronia* was employed in the coastal trade, transporting cargo to the many outport communities strung along the coast of Newfoundland. On this evening, the captain and his crew rowed ashore from their vessel that had been moored safely in the middle of the harbour. They were intent on a good meal and perhaps a pint of refreshment in one of the many drinking establishments on Water Street. At 9 pm, the captain and his first mate returned to their dory and began their short row out to midstream. They were dumbfounded when they reached the spot where they had left their *Veronia*. She was gone! Another schooner had just arrived, and was preparing her mooring nearby. The Captain hailed her crew and asked if they had seen his ship. They responded by saying that they had indeed passed the *Veronia* just outside Fort Amherst. She apparently was travelling at a good clip straight out to sea.

The wayward *Veronia* was found the next day unmanned and adrift off Cape Spear. Amazing as it may seem, her mooring must have come loose, and caught in the outgoing tide, managed to pass through the "Narrows" unscathed.

The hectic years during World War I saw much activity in the port of St. John's. Many troopships departed from King's Wharf to pass by the old Fort Amherst lighthouse on their way to ports in Britain and France. They were carrying the courageous Royal Newfoundland Regiment bound for glory and, for many, death on foreign battlefields.

There was a relative lull in port activity after the War years. This lull continued in the 1920s, as the Newfoundland economy was pulled down by the declining price of cod. Captain Robert Sheppard had taken over from his grandfather, Austin Sheppard, during this time. Austin's son, John, had died at sea years before, and so the job was passed on to his son, Robert.

Early in the morning of July 2, 1933, there was too much traffic in the Narrows for the liking of Captain Williams of the SS *Marsland*. She was a 4,500 ton British freighter that had departed from Cadiz loaded

"Fort Amherst and SS Rosiland, 1920s."

with a cargo of fishery salt bound for St. John's. In the early morning light, the crew prepared to take her through the Narrows. Robert Sheppard watched in disbelief as a small schooner worked its way out of the Narrows. The little boat darted past the *Marslands*, tacking right in front of the ship. Captain Williams ordered the ship full reverse, swerving to avoid collision with the errant schooner. They managed to miss it but drove the freighter high up on a sunken shoal known as the Vestral Rocks, just below Fort Amherst lighthouse. This was a spectacular scene, with the large 400-foot freighter pinned to rocks at the entrance to the harbour.

The crew began to dump the valuable salt cargo in an effort to refloat the stricken ship. The Railway ships *Meigle* and *Argyle* attempted to tow her off the shoal, but their lines parted with each try. As the sea ground the large freighter on the jagged rocks, the ship's holds were punctured one by one and she began to fill with water. The powerful sea tug, *Foundation Franklin*, arrived a week later and attempted to pump sea water out of the flooded holds. All efforts failed. Finally, a strong southeast gale blew up, and her fate was sealed. The heavy seas pounded her hull; she was declared a complete wreck. The *Marsland* was stripped of her valuable fittings and equipment. Throughout the summer and into the fall, the wreck remained firmly aground on the shoal below Fort Amherst.

The Port Authority was at a loss to figure how to rid themselves of the wreck. They even considered contracting the British warship, HMS

Norfolk due for a visit, to blow her out of the harbour entrance. The sea mercifully took care of the job. Quietly one night in the fall, the old freighter slipped off the shoal and sank in deeper water beyond the entrance.

In the 1934, Captain Sheppard and his wife Sadie received permission to open the "Narrows Tea Room" in the large shed building located just east of the stone lighthouse. This little restaurant business was intended to supplement Sheppard's modest salary. The unique and scenic location made it a popular retreat for the inhabitants of the town. They operated it successfully until 1939 when World War II intervened.

With the outbreak of war that fall, it was decided that St. John's would again serve as an important collecting point for convoys and warships departing for Britain. In December 1940, the Canadian Department of National Defence officially took over Fort Amherst for use as a Naval Signal Station and barracks. Ninety men were stationed at Fort Amherst for the next seven years. They also took the time to re-arm the entrance to St. John's harbour. The Canadian government installed two twenty-foot artillery pieces on the cliffs below the old fort.

Captain Sheppard abruptly resigned as head lighthouse keeper at Fort Amherst at the start of the war. He began a more daring career, taking requisitioned merchant ships overseas for the British Admiralty. Ben Dalton was brought in to operate Fort Amherst lighthouse. He occupied the very cold and damp stone building with his wife and five children.

The waters around St. John's and Conception Bay teemed with German submarines during the war years. They were intent on mining the harbour area, trying to sink any merchant shipping they could find. In the afternoon of March 3, 1941, a German sub lying off the harbour entrance fired a torpedo at an old steamer entering the harbour. They had hoped to sink her, effectively blocking the harbour. The torpedo missed the ship and exploded on the red sandstone cliff right below the lighthouse. A second torpedo was caught without exploding in the submarine net strung across the Narrows at Chain Rock. This incident had a frightening effect on Ben Dalton's wife. There had always been a possibility that a submarine could surface and try to strafe the building, attempting to put the lighthouse out of action. His family was quickly moved into town.

In 1943, an American freighter and a British ore carrier were lost to mines outside the harbour. After the war a German submarine did manage to get by the guns at Fort Amherst. The *U-190* surrendered to the frigate HMCS *Victoriaville* at sea off Bay Bulls on May 12, 1945. She entered St. John's harbour, passing below Fort Amherst early on the morning of June 3. The periscope is all that remains of the *U-190*; this is mounted on the wall at the Crow's Nest, a popular watering hole during and after the war.

In the same year, a new assistant was appointed at Fort Amherst. Leo Power, with his wife and large family, moved into the old lighthouse. This arrangement proved difficult. The building had been poorly maintained during the war years and had very badly deteriorated. When the Royal Canadian Navy vacated their barracks in 1946, Mr. Power promptly moved his eleven children into the building. Three years later, Dalton retired and Leo Power became the sixth keeper at Fort Amherst.

In 1947, the old lighthouse was returned first to the Newfoundland government and later to the Canadian Department of Transportation. The old stone building had suffered the ravages of Newfoundland weather, and countless shattering explosive charges marking the hours of a hundred years. In 1952, the lighthouse was demolished to make way for a modest twelve-foot-high wooden structure. Two bungalows, one for Leo Power's family, the other for his assistant Conn Bennett were also built. An electric 500W lamp was installed inside a dioptric drum lens to light the entrance to St. John's harbour.

Very little has changed in the forty years since then. Leo Power retired in November, 1972. Conn Bennett became the last keeper at Fort Amherst. When he retired in 1983, the station was made automatic. Today it is frequented by tourists hoping for a glimpse of an iceberg on its southward journey in the spring. A group of "townies" may find their way out the narrow Southside Road in hopes of escaping the bustle of Water Street for the solitude of South Head.

To visit Fort Amherst, you should travel down the west end of Water Street. Take the interchange off Water Street that crosses over the Waterford River. The intersection across the river is formed by Southside Road and Blackhead Road that runs straight up Southside Hill to Shea Heights and beyond to Cape Spear. Turn left and run about 3.5 km east on Southside Road as it skirts along the edge of the harbour below the 400-foot hill. You should note the Newfoundland Drydock on the left and the old site of the parish church of St. Mary the Virgin on the right. You will drive past the Coast Guard Station with its red and white icebreakers docked alongside. This is near the site where the Newfoundland Squadron of the British Navy docked their great wooden warships in the eighteenth and nineteenth centuries. Just beyond you will notice an area of rotting piers; it was these piers that served the great sealing fleets of the nineteenth century. Ships commanded by such well known Newfoundland sea captains as Kean and Bartlett tied up here. These men were famous sealing captains who went out onto the icefields that formed each spring off the northeast coast of Newfoundland.

Baine, Johnston and Company, Job Brothers and Bowring Brothers, all great merchant houses, had wharfs here. During the Second World War, the Royal Canadian Navy tied their corvettes and destroyers here. You can still see the subterranean mines cut in the red sandstone across from the fish plant, used to house ammunition during the war.

As you turn the corner of the harbour and head east along what is known as the Narrows you will pass around an electrical generating plant built in 1956. Paul O'Neil describes it as "A power plant of repulsive aspect squat(ing) like a bloated frog on the southside of the Narrows." This is an apt description. Just beyond the Prowser's Rock Small Boat Facility, you should notice a brief rise or knoll. There you will find an area covered in white sand bags and enclosed in a high steel fence. This is what remains of the Southside Castle built in the 1660s. It was made famous by the heroic resistance of the townsfolk during the French siege of 1705.

Park your car there and walk through the village of Fort Amherst where descendants of the first settlers still live. Watch for the white plaque that commemorates the Frederick Battery built in 1812 to help strengthen the harbour from attack by American privateers. If you scramble up over the bank, you can see what remains of the battery's foundation. The sandstone stone is shaped and dressed with a precision that you would not see today.

Walk up the last one hundred metres to the place where the lighthouse is built, one hundred and ten feet above the level of the sea. The view of Signal Hill, towering above the harbour entrance is staggering. The view back toward the safe inner harbour is the same that greeted the earliest explorers five hundred years ago.

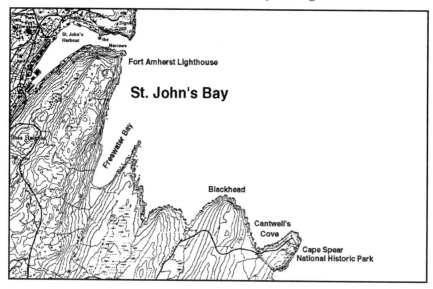

Cape Spear
(eclipse 2.6 sec.; flash 0.4 sec., eclipse 8.6 sec.)

The Easterly Light

The rocky ledge runs far into the sea,
and on its outer point, some miles away,
The Lighthouse lifts its massive masonry,
A pillar of fire by night, of cloud by day.

from Henry Longfellow's *The Lighthouse*

From the heights of Signal Hill, you can look east toward Ireland. In the distance, a low barren headland runs parallel to the horizon. From that headland to Cape Clear on the southwestern most corner of Ireland is 1650 miles clear sailing, the New World's closest point to the Old. On a clear day, on the crown of this distant headland, you can see the Cape Spear Light, Newfoundland's oldest existing lighthouse.

Cape Spear is a corruption of the french noun *esperance* or *hope*. The early explorers, after completing the long crossing of the Atlantic Ocean, were probably expressing their emotions upon first sighting the Cape. The earliest maps, dating from just after Cabot's discovery, show it as Cape d'Espera. In 1527, John Rut, the English navigator, mentions Cape de Sper in his letter to Henry VII. This distinctive promontory helped to mark the harbour of St. John's which lay hidden just beyond. Because Cape Spear was difficult to approach by sea and was isolated from the

51

W.F. Rennie for Canadian Illustrated News, May 6, 1871.

"View of Cape Spear from Signal Hill."

main road running south to Bay Bulls, it remained uninhabited into the nineteenth century.

With the rise in sea traffic around the entrance to St. John's harbour, it became clear to Governor Thomas Cochrane in the early 1830s that his government should consider establishing a light at Cape Spear. Cochrane reasoned that "an ordinary light and a heavy gun would no doubt prove of great advantage to the trade." He personally visited Cape Spear in the spring of 1834 and chose the final site. It was to perch high atop the Cape at the very edge of a vertical 240-foot sandstone cliff.

In the first session of the Newfoundland House of Assembly, the members passed a bill giving permission for the young Colony to borrow £1,000 that would be used to build the lighthouse. This is the earliest record of the Newfoundland government's raising money by a loan for use in the construction of a public building. Work began on the foundation in the summer of 1834. The firm of Croake and Parker was contracted to build the lighthouse for the sum of £440. The design was based on similar plans developed by the Northern Light House Board in Scotland. It was used again several years later on Harbour Grace Island. A simple two-storey house was constructed for the keeper, his family and his assistant. Unfortunately, this wood frame house was built fairly lightly. The nature of the construction would have disastrous effect a decade later. The exterior of the house reflected the clean simple lines of the Regency style, an architectural form that was popular in Britain at the time. The architect indicated false windows opposite real windows in the façade of the house. This curious detail was said to give the lighthouse a pleasing symmetrical appearance. A thirty-five-foot-high, circular stone tower rose through the centre of the house, anchoring the structure to the red sandstone cliff.

The lighthouse was completed during the following summer. The lantern room was designed by the firm of Robert Stevenson and Sons. It was to be ten feet in diameter, framed in wood and covered by a copper dome. Eight silvered copper reflectors complete with Argand lamps were set in a gunmetal frame. The apparatus revolved at one minute intervals. This twenty-year-old light mechanism came from Inchkeith Lighthouse on the Firth of Forth in Scotland. It was refurbished by the Scottish firm of McBride and Kerr at a cost of £628. Because of its height above sea level, the light could be seen for a distance of 36 miles.

Out in the bay between Cape Spear and St. John's, a drama took place that summer that was to have an impact on the Cape Spear lighthouse to this very day. In July of 1835, all of St. John's was anxiously waiting for the arrival of the Crown Prince of the Netherlands. Prince Henry was to make a Royal Visit on board the frigate *Rhine*. On the day the warship neared the Newfoundland coast off St. John's, she was enveloped in a dense fog. The Governor dispatched several pilot boats in search of the lost Prince and his ship.

A young harbour pilot named James Cantwell managed to find the ship and guide her through the Narrows to the safety of St. John's harbour. Prince Henry wanted to grant a favour to Cantwell for his able assistance in guiding the Dutch ship into port. Cantwell knew that the Cape Spear lighthouse was under construction; he asked to become the lighthouse keeper there. The job had already been given to another man, Emanuel Warre, so it would be another ten years before Prince Henry's decree would come into effect.

Cape Spear lighthouse was lit for the first time on September 1, 1836. The merchant houses of St. John's immediately hailed it for its assistance to their shipping entering and leaving the port. From the hill at Cape Spear, you can look west back towards St. John's. While the town is obscured by the high Southside Hills, you can just make out the small white triangle that is Fort Amherst. Signal Hill, with the stone tower at its summit, can be made out just to the right of Fort Amherst. The merchant houses quickly devised a plan to take advantage of Cape Spear's unique location just within sighting distance from St. John's. They erected a high yardarm behind the lighthouse and another on top of Signal Hill. It would be one of the tasks of the keeper to scan the horizon for inbound shipping. Each ship carried on her mast the distinctive house flag of the company which owned her. Warre was to run the same flag up his own mast. The garrison atop Signal Hill was to monitor the Cape Spear lighthouse. They were to respond to Warre's signals simultaneously by running the same flag up the wooden Blockhouse located there. In this way the merchant firms, comfortable in their offices on Water Street, could get early warning of the arrival of one of their ships. This practice of signals was so effective that they would continue it for nearly one hundred and twenty years. It also gave Signal Hill its name.

With Emmanuel Warre's death in 1845, James Cantwell took over as the second keeper at Cape Spear. He brought with him his wife Elizabeth and ten children to the cramped wooden lighthouse on that windswept cliff. Elizabeth had been a Manning, her mother a Molloy from Trepassey. Right away, the Cantwells had misgivings about the strength of the structure; ten years of powerful winter storms had loosened the wooden joints of the house. Nevertheless, they settled into the peaceful routine that should have been broken only by the quiet change of the seasons and the occasional visit by the supply vessel bringing provisions.

Their peace would be shattered within a year after they moved in. In September 1846, a tremendous hurricane struck the east coast of Newfoundland. It would effectively demolish the frail wooden lighthouse at Cape Spear. In the height of the storm, with his family huddled in the kitchen, Cantwell watched as one side of the house lifted several inches off its foundation. In a report to the House of Assembly that followed the accident, the Inspector wrote..."the memorable gale of September 19th, which blew there with such violence...shook the frame-work of the light-room...as to crack every pane of glass in the lantern, and rendered the whole tremulous and infirm ever since..." They gave Nicholas Croake, the original contractor, the task of rebuilding the lighthouse at a cost of £484. This figure was actually more than the original contract. As an added precaution against the destructive influence of the high winds at Cape Spear, they instructed Croake to install heavy chains on the four corners of the lighthouse, anchoring them in the sandstone. This lighthouse would suffer repeatedly from damage caused by wind storms in the years to follow.

In the spring of each year, pan ice drifts slowly southward from Baffin Island and Greenland to the east coast of Newfoundland. This pan ice forms a solid impenetrable mass that grinds and rafts up high along this coast. Strangely, it was this pan ice that would cause more accidents off Cape Spear than that caused by the heavy fogs. On Monday, April 1, 1856, the brigantine *Heather*, eight days out of Baltimore, encountered heavy ice and a heavy sea off Cape Spear. She was bound for the Baine, Johnston & Company wharf on the Southside. Her captain was Richard Ash. He was born at Trinity and had spent his life on the high seas. Throughout the day, the square rigger attempted to work its way through the pan ice on its way to St. John's. A northerly wind blew up and closed the ice in around the *Heather*. She was trapped and blowing onshore. The crew was terrified. At 6 pm that evening, they approached Captain Ash and asked if they could abandon the ship. The welcoming light of Cape Spear shone only a half mile away. The sea swells were so large that Captain Ash reasoned that proceeding across the ice would be too dangerous. He felt that they would never make it to shore. Also, he hated the idea of abandoning his precious ship. Four of his crew wouldn't listen to him. They set out across the ice for Cape Spear safely making it at nightfall. James Cantwell and his oldest son, Dennis, were waiting on shore, to help them up the steep hill to the warm kitchen in the lighthouse.

The two remaining crew, the first mate and the Captain did not fare as well. The wind freshened into a gale, and the stricken vessel caught in the ice continued to drift towards the sheer cliff at Cape Spear. They could wait no longer, they leapt onto one large pan, just minutes before the ship was dashed into matchsticks on the cliff.

The next morning all that was left of the *Heather* was a few shattered timbers left high on the rocks by the huge sea. Cantwell feared the worse. He reported that the men had been lost using the new signalling system. Miraculously, Captain Ash and his men were still alive; the ice pan with the four men clinging to it did not meet the same fate as the ship. It drifted southward parallel to the coast all that night. The morning dawned with the men miserably cold but alive. They watched as the Southern Shore of the Avalon Peninsula slipped slowly past their right hand. They drifted all Tuesday and Wednesday. It must have been another miracle, because on Wednesday evening, the residents of Ferryland, 32 miles south of Cape Spear, sighted the shipwrecked men offshore. A boat with ten fishermen aboard rowed out to attempt a rescue. They succeeded in reaching the ice pan which carried the men. The rescuers brought Captain Ash and his men on board the little boat.

But then the story took another twist. The northerly wind veered off to the west, blowing the small boat further offshore. They finally reached land the following night after rowing hard in a headwind for twenty-four hours. There was quite a celebration when the townsfolk of St. John's realized that their Captain Ash had returned to them back from the dead.

Four years later, the crew of the brigantine *Salmah* was not as lucky. In late October of that year, the *Salmah* had departed from New York with cargo for Halifax and St. John's. It was late in the evening of November 16 when the *Salmah* arrived off St. John's. At midnight the wind died away completely and the ship was becalmed. The tide began to carry the vessel close to the rocks on the eastern side of Cape Spear. Captain James Crowe ordered his crew to anchor the ship bow and stern to prevent her drifting any closer to the cliff. During the night a strong northeast wind came up, the anchor chains parted and the *Salmah* drove hard onto the rocks at the very point of Cape Spear. They attempted to get a boat over the side, but it was crushed against the side of the ship in the heavy seas. Soon the ship itself began to break up. The *Salmah* was close enough to shore for Cantwell to throw a small line on board. They quickly passed a heavier line ashore and rigged up a bosun's chair. Most of the crew got ashore by this method. During the transfer two men and a boy were carried away in the pounding surf. Just as the last man got off, the wooden ship was crushed by the sea and was gone.

In the 1860s, Inspector Oke began to consider the merits of different types of fog alarm for Cape Spear with their engineers in Scotland. While they were recommending a bell, Oke perferred the idea of a steam whistle. They even considered the possibility of relocating the Fort Amherst dynamite gun. This idea was eventually declined: "The serious danger likely to arise from moving a long established signal, one so well known as this gun, to a new station, is a very strong objection to this plan." They figured that it would confuse mariners attempting to enter port. Also, they realized that they would have to move the small contingent of soldiers out to the Cape to operate the gun, a very expensive proposition.

By now Cantwell's children all had grown and most had moved to St. John's. Dennis Cantwell had remained with his father as assistant keeper at Cape Spear. Dennis had married Mary Carrol in late 1850s. In 1865, the Lighthouse Service put a substantial extension on the east side of the lighthouse to accommodate his growing family - there would eventually be ten children. This was the first of many additions and alterations that would be made to the structure.

The light burners were converted to kerosene in 1874. Inspector Nevill suggested, "The change has increased the brilliance of the light - in fact so much so that the keeper at Ferryland Head remarked the change from his station." A more brilliant light did not help the Spanish brigantine *Mayaquzanna* one dark night two years later off Cape Spear.

The summer of 1876 had been very hot and dry. By mid August a huge fire had started in the forests on the shore of Conception Bay near Kelligrews and Seal Cove. Uncontrolled, it smouldered and smoked for weeks. The wind was such that the dense smoke was blown eastward across the peninsula, to envelop St. John's and the bay beyond.

Late on the evening of August 14, the great square-rigger *Mayaquzanna* made the entrance of St. John's harbour. She had departed from the West Indies loaded with a cargo of sugar and molasses. Captain Fiol signalled for a pilot to come out and assist the ship through the Narrows. Signal Hill responded but because the smoke prevented the signal from being seen in the pilot office - no boat was sent. The Spanish captain, lost in the blackness of that smoky night, brought his ship about to sail east across St. John's Bay toward Cape Spear. He was satisfied to wait until morning when the visibility would improve.

Unfortunately, Captain Fiol, his wife and nine year old daughter died in the surf off Blackhead just west of Cape Spear. With the lighthouse at Cape Spear obscured by the thick smoke, the *Mayaquzanna* crashed into the sheer cliff only one mile west of the lighthouse.

The following spring, work began preparing a site for a fog alarm at Cape Spear. It was to be a steam whistle similar to the one at Cape Race built in 1872. This new steam whistle needed a ready source of water to supply the boiler. This posed quite a problem at Cape Spear, since the entire cape was one massive red sandstone cliff. It was the rocky hill that eventually provided a solution - a solution that would work only some of the time. Well below the lighthouse running towards the very point of the cape, a number of rocky hollows and small bogs constantly collected rainwater. Using a system of ditches and buried iron pipe, they were able to supply the fog alarm with water using gravity. The building was built below this collecting area on the hill very near the present site of the fog alarm. The site commanded an excellent view of St. John's Bay. Unfortunately, the system proved quite ineffective. It froze up solidly in the winter and often dried up in the summer. Later, a large brick cistern was build next to the fog alarm building. Even then, during dry spells, Cantwell and his family had to cart water from the brook some distance away.

The fog alarm worked well for sea traffic in St. John's Bay, but because it was located below the crest of the hill, mariners approaching from the south could not hear it at all. There were immediate calls to construct a second fog alarm turned to the south.

The old lighthouse was renovated during the construction of the fog alarm, taking advantage of the carpenters who had been sent out for that purpose. The site was very exposed, "the shingling of the roofs suffered severely from gales of wind, many patches of the outer coat having been blown away. The nails are so eaten away as to have no hold of the rough board."

"During the past year (1880), the lighthouse department lost a very old and generally esteemed servant, James Cantwell, who for 35 years discharged the duties of this station in such a way as to maintain the high character of the light he had in charge," so wrote Inspector Nevill in his report to the House of Assembly in 1881. Dennis, who had assisted his father for many years, took over as head keeper. He would remain in that position for nearly as long as his father.

In 1897, after considerable lobbying from the St. John's merchants, a second steam whistle was built at Cape Spear. It was located about four hundred metres southwest of the old lighthouse, on the cliffs looking south towards Petty Harbour. In heavy fog, both alarms sounded simultaneously. This proved to be an expensive proposition for the Lighthouse Service both in terms of materials and labour. The steam boilers consumed 60 to 80 tons of coal annually. As there was no road connecting the station to St. John's, the construction of a substantial supply wharf in the small cove west of the cape was started.

Problems, particularly with the eastward fog alarm, continued. With the developments of the diaphone driven by a diesel motor, Inspector White began to lobby the government for the replacement of the aging and troublesome fog alarm. This took place in 1909; the new one was built 140 metres straight below the old site. Unfortunately, they built it a bit too close to the sea. In severe winter storms, the heavy seas would wash around the very foundations of the building.

Dennis Cantwell died that same year, having operated the Cape Spear lighthouse for twenty-nine years. He had assisted his father for the thirty years before that. Dennis's eldest son became the new keeper at Cape Spear. James Cantwell II was fifty years old. His brother, William, became his assistant. A third keeper was hired to assist the two brothers in the operation of the light and the two fog alarms.

That spring had been a bad one for icebergs. It was in June that another unusual marine accident took place off Cape Spear. The English schooner, *Geisha*, had been employed in the Newfoundland trade for only two years. On the sixth of June, after a twenty-five-day crossing from Cadiz, she encountered pack ice and bergs off the Newfoundland coast. That evening, the *Giesha* struck an iceberg that carried away her bowsprit, jib boom and most of her sails forward. Later that night, having lost much of her ability to manoeuvre, the stricken *Giesha* crashed into a second iceberg only two miles east of Cape Spear. The crew realized the imminent disaster. They managed to climb into a lifeboat just before she struck. The mass of the schooner shifted the iceberg's centre of gravity. In the darkness the enormous iceberg, larger than a ten-storey building, rolled, smashing the one hundred and thirty ton schooner like an egg shell. Amazingly, the crew in the lifeboat had rowed far enough away to avoid being dragged down by the wall of ice. They began rowing for shore and were eventually picked up by a passing ship later in the morning.

After one hundred years of operation, the old catoptric light mechanism first used at Inchkeith began to show its age. In 1912, Inspector White recommended that this light mechanism be replaced. A new dioptric mechanism using kerosene was installed. A couple of years later, acetylene gas was substituted as the illuminant because of its excellent properties. Sixteen years later, electric incandescent lamps were installed.

James Cantwell died in 1918, only nine years after taking over from his father Dennis. He had seven sons, and over the next quarter century, four of his sons would have a hand in operating the lighthouse at Cape Spear.

Engraved by Shell & Hogan for *Harper's Weekly*, June 12, 1880.

"An Iceberg encounter."

William had been the oldest and had assisted his father in the early days of the twentieth century. He became the keeper in the early 1920s with the assistance of his two younger brothers Jack and Weston. Unfortunately, William did not remain as keeper for very long. Whether it was a stroke or a form of Alzheimer's disease, William became too ill to carry on, retiring officially in 1930. He died several years later.

Jack was the next oldest; he operated the lighthouse in the early thirties. It was during this time a near fatal accident took place at Cape Spear. Jack would be credited for having saved the lives of two of his younger brothers. The fog alarm that had been built down below the heights of the Cape, had always been criticized by the keepers. They had complained that it was too exposed to the full force of the northeast winter storms. It was one such tormented night that found Wes and his youngest brother Michael down in the "Whistle House". They were preparing the station for a long stormy night. They decided to leave the windows of the building closed for fear that even a crack in the windows would cause them to be wrecked by the savage winds and sea spray. What they didn't realize was that the diesel engine was slowly consuming the precious oxygen in the air. At the same time, the engine was giving off the deadly carbon monoxide gas. They slowly succumbed to this invisible poison, passing out on the floor of the building.

Safe and snug in the large rambling lighthouse up on the crest of the hill, Weston's wife had become anxious over the lateness of her husband's return. Finally, they could wait no longer. Jack and the woman began the perilous journey down the face of the cliff in the height of the storm, hauling themselves hand over hand on a safety rope. They made it to the whistle house. Opening the iron door, they found the two men unconscious and barely breathing. Jack dragged his brothers to the door, with the seas breaking just beneath the building. A few more minutes, both men would have died. Weston revived and recovered after many days. Michael was not as lucky. He never really recovered from the accident, and died two years later.

Jack remained as keeper through the early 1930s, but as the years passed, he tired of the lonely life and eventually decided to resign and move his family into St. John's. Wes took over from his brother and operated the lighthouse in the late 1930s and throughout most of the War years.

Those years of peaceful existence that the Cantwell brothers and their families had known was to be shattered at the start of World War II. In 1940, the American and Royal Canadian Navies had grown concerned over the presence of German U-boats. Both St. John's and Bay Bulls harbours had become a hub for convoys preparing to make their way east across the Atlantic to Britain. The area had already attracted this hidden submarine menace. They resolved to build a powerful coastal battery. It was their intention to defend the Allied shipping that sailed the seas around St. John's Bay.

The Canadian Government acquired two enormous breech-loading cannons cast in a foundry in the United States fifty years before. Each thirty-foot artillery piece weighed over fifty tons. After landing at the community of Blackhead, they were dragged overland to the very tip of Cape Spear. Each gun was supported on a steel carriage. Using counter weights, they could swing the gun into position after loading. The shells, weighing nearly 600 pounds, could be fired as far as eight miles to sea. Weston complained that when one of the guns did go off, the foundation of the lighthouse shook so badly that the teacups would be knocked out of the cupboard. The 103rd Coastal Defence Battery of the Royal Canadian Artillery was stationed there during the war to operate the two guns buried in the red sandstone cliffs of Cape Spear. During the war years, the lighthouse station housed quite a contingent of soldiers. They built a large barracks and mess hall complete with a little movie theatre and chapel. These buildings occupied the present day site of the parking lot. The battery never saw action; they never fired the great guns in defence of the harbour. Ironically, several soldiers died there in swimming accidents. Another man died on board a Canadian warship that ran straight in to the vertical cliffs just below the lighthouse during one black night.

During the War, Wes was instructed to observe blackout conditions in an effort to foil the German efforts to locate St. John's harbour. After over one hundred years of ceaseless operation, the light was extinguished for long periods of time. Wes maintained radio communication with military intelligence in St. John's. When a convoy was expected to pass, he would receive a coded message. In response, he was to operate the light for several prescribed hours.

Weston's wife passed away in 1943. He was deeply saddened by her death. Not wanting to raise his family alone at Cape Spear, he decided to resign and move to St. John's. In July 1944, twenty-six year old Frank Cantwell was appointed the head keeper at Cape Spear. He was the fourth brother in his family and had been living in Central Newfoundland with his new wife Margret. Although he had grown up at Cape Spear, Frank Cantwell never really expected to be called upon to operate the station. In the end he would be in charge of the Cape Spear Lighthouse the longest, a total of twenty-six years.

With the rapid development of new technologies for navigational aids after the War, it was decided that the old antiquated lighthouse, now nearly one hundred and twenty years old, should be replaced. In 1952, a new reinforced concrete tower was built down below the old site. The 1912 light mechanism was transferred to the new tower. Two bungalows were built to accommodate Frank Cantwell, his family and the assistant keeper's family. Mr. Cantwell passed away in 1972. His eldest son, Gerry, became the new keeper, the eighth Cantwell to have that responsibility.

By the late 1970s, the old structure had been abandoned. Vandals had begun breaking into the building, stealing what ever they could find. The Department of Transportation decided to demolish the historic lighthouse. Before that fate befell the lighthouse, and after a considerable lobby by heritage conservation groups in St. John's, the site was designated a National Historic Site. In the early 1980s, work began by historians and architects working with Parks Canada to restore the building to its original plan. During the visit of Prince Charles and Lady

"Cape Spear before renovations."

Diana in June 1983, the splendid building and site were opened to the public.

To get to Cape Spear, travel to the west end of Water Street, taking the same turn as you did for Fort Amherst. Drive up Southside Hill, passing through the suburban community of Shea Heights. From the summit, you can witness a spectacular view of St. John's. You can expect a fifteen minute drive eastward out toward Cape Spear. The rolling hills of this coastal area is marked only once by the community of Blackhead. The little church in the community was built by its residents around the same time the lighthouse was built. Two lighthouse keepers are buried in the cemetery, that can be found below the church. Thickets of blueberry bushes grow between the white stones.

As you clear the last headland and head out across the barren cape, the silhouette of the twin lighthouses can be seen on the horizon. On the crown of the hill is the original lighthouse, just to the left below is the concrete lighthouse built in the 1950s. From the car park there is an excellent wooden stair that takes the visitor up to the present lighthouse. A small museum located directly opposite the concrete tower is open during the summer months. Walk to James Cantwell's lighthouse just one hundred metres beyond.

The National Park has a number of very accessible walking trails. One trail takes you down the cliff face to the abandoned ruins of the World War II gun emplacement. From here, it is a very brief walk to the very tip of the Cape. It is in fact the most easterly point of North America.

Cape Bonavista
(Flash 0.5 seconds; eclipse 9.5 seconds)
Cabot's Light

"The said Messer Zoanne(Cabot), as he is a foreigner and poor, would not be believed if his partners who are all Englishmen, and from Bristol, did not testify to the truth of what he tells. This Messer Zoanne has the description of the world in a chart, and also in a solid globe which he has made, and he shows where he landed; and that going toward the east he passed considerably beyond the country of the Tannias...."

from a letter by Riamondo di Soncino
to the Duke of Milan, December, 1497

Tradition has it that on the morning of June 24, 1497, a small sailing ship named the *Matthew* came within sight of a narrow headland on the northeast coast of Newfoundland. The captain of the ship, an Italian from Venice, is said to have exclaimed, "Oh...buona vista!"— what a beautiful sight! Zoanne (John) Cabotto with a crew of eighteen, had departed from the English port of Bristol a month before, on a voyage to find the northern route to the Spice Islands of the Far East. Henry VII had heard of the amazing discoveries of Christopher Columbus commissioned by the Spanish King five years before. He had sent John Cabot, a country man of Columbus, to erect the Royal Standard of the English nation on any lands that he should discover during his travels.

Several years later, Juan de la Cosa, a map maker, who had been Columbus's pilot, completed a map which showed the great discoveries of his master. His map clearly showed the coastline of Florida and the location of many of the islands of the West Indies. On the top of his map away to the north, la Cosa showed a long, straight coastline that ran eastward to a point whereupon it turned abruptly northward. Along this coastline he inscribed the notation, "Mar Descubierta por Ingleses," or "sea discovered by the English." He showed the prominent cape as "Cavo de Ynglaterra" or "Cape English." It is believed that John Cabot had travelled to Seville and Lisbon after his return from the New World. He may have met la Cosa, and passed on details of his discoveries. Many feel that the outline shown on la Cosa's map represents the south coast of Newfoundland, with Cape English actually Cape Race.

The first detailed map of Newfoundland was prepared by John Mason, an experienced captain in the Royal Navy. He had been the Governor of Cupids in Conception Bay during the mid-1620s. Many major bays and headlands are shown on this old map. Opposite Cape Bonavista he wrote, "A Caboto primum reperta" - "First found by Cabot."

In 1534, Jacques Cartier made his first landfall at Cape Bonavista much in the same way Cabot had found it thirty years before. He had departed on April 20 from St. Malo in France sailing northeasterly. His little ship, caught in the northern currents and having a good wind, made "Cap de Bonaviste" as he called it in the record time of twenty days. He then travelled northward to the Strait of Belle Isle and went on to discover the Gulf of St. Lawrence. The replication of Cabot's trip demonstrates a maritime tradition that is still recognized today. Departing in the spring, headed northwestward from Europe or Great Britain, with the prevailing westerlies, you invariably would strike the northeastern coast of Newfoundland.

The claim that Cape Bonavista was the actual site of Cabot's first landfall has been contested by some proponents in Cape Breton. Much of the controversy is based on a map inscribed with the name "Sebastian" that turned up in Germany in 1843. It is believed to have been prepared by John Cabot's son. Sebastian had indeed travelled with his father as a boy to the New World. The map shows a headland that looks much like that of Cape Breton. The words "terra prima vista" are indicated beside the headland. The map also shows many landmarks and features discovered and named by Cartier. It is important to understand that, by the 1540s, the French began to colonize Canada. Many believe that Sebastian Cabot, hoping to ingratiate himself with the English, had shown his father's discovery to be on Cape Breton rather than Cape

Bonavista. He did this in hopes of strengthening the English claim on that territory.

This map, known as the "Cabot Map," is most often mentioned in the controversy over Cabot's first landfall. It is more than likely that the controversy will never be settled. When you consider a map of the North Atlantic and location of the island of Newfoundland, it is hard to believe that Cabot's little ship could have passed by the north and eastern coasts of Newfoundland without detecting it.

After those early years of discovery, the English were attracted by the excellent fishing off the northeastern coast of Newfoundland. They began to settle in many of its protected bays and inlets. They were pursuing the salt fish trade with Britain and New England. Early in the seventeenth century, some fishermen had built their simple homes in one shallow bay in particular. It was located just south of Cape Bonavista on the west side of the peninsula. While it was exposed to the winter winds, the bay did have a good source of fresh water that ran from a hill to a fertile estuary known as Mockbeggar Cove. The town would eventually come to be known as Bonavista, named after the famous headland nearby. The town would form the northern boundary of the "English Shore," which ran southeast past Conception Bay, on to St. John's and Ferryland. In 1677, Bonavista had eighteen houses to St. John's forty-five, making it the second most populated community in Newfoundland.

In the 1690s, the whole of the English Shore was terrorized by the French from their stronghold in Placentia. After Commander d'Ibberville's destruction of St. John's in 1696, the English built three small forts in Bonavista. Eight years later the settlers in Bonavista would have to defend themselves against a French attack. A New England fishing trader named Michael Gill had spent the summer of 1704 in Bonavista. He intended to fill the holds of his ships with salt cod for the residents of Boston and New York. Aware of the hostilities between England and France, he had brought a fourteen-gun sloop to defend against privateers.

At two in the morning of August 18, two French sloops, loaded with marines, slipped into Bonavista harbour. They were led by Commander La Grange who had served under d'Ibberville. They had hoped to destroy the English merchant ships there under the cover of darkness before the English garrison stationed at the nearby fort on Green Island could respond. As the French began to bombard the ships, Gill engaged them with his lone warship. Outnumbered two to one, Gill held them off for six hours. At daybreak, the townsfolk began to return fire from shore. The French invaders retreated out to sea.

La Grange attacked again later in the fall. Unfortunately, there were no ships to defend the fishing families this time. Gill's company ships had already returned to New England. The French captured and burned several large English merchantmen that were fully loaded for their trip to England that autumn. The English garrison arrived from Green Island the next morning but the French had already departed.

During the winter the English garrison returned to St. John's. Early in the spring the French made one last attack on Bonavista. The French privateers were lead by Monsieur de Montigny. After the recent attack, the English settlers lacked stomach to stand and defend Bonavista from the little fort at Mockbeggar Cove. They fled in small boats to the fort at Green Island. This modest, wooden fort was equipped with nine small cannons. It was located on a small grassy island which lay north of the community just south of Cape Bonavista, only a stone's throw from shore. They were led by a prominent resident of Bonavista, George Skiffington, a Quaker. As the French warships began to shell the fort, Skiffington surrendered. He figured that paying a ransom was more sensible than fighting it out with the French. The French departed £4,500 richer, without destroying the town.

With the Treaty of Utrecht, the French yielded Placentia. They were given fishing rights for a portion of the Newfoundland coastline that would run from Cape Bonavista to Pointe Riche on the west coast. After that the migratory life of the West Country fishermen and merchants stabilized, and the population increased significantly. By 1725, there were about three hundred people living in Bonavista. The community had a school and a church with a fulltime minister.

Later, the cod fishery would be complemented by the excellent seal fishery that took place from Bonavista. The fishermen would depart in the spring of each year in small open boats. They were hunting for harp seals that were whelping their pups on the pan ice that had drifted close to shore. The seal carcasses would serve as an excellent source of protein for the settlers when most of their winter supplies had been depleted. The skins and the oil were processed and sold to traders in St. John's and England providing cash to outfit for the fishing season that would follow. It would be the combination of these two activities that made Bonavista one of the largest and strongest economically of all the towns on the English shore.

By the 1840s, the population of the town had grown to two thousand people. The Colonial Government had become well aware of the increased marine traffic in the Bonavista and Trinity Bays. The Lighthouse Board had hoped to assist fishermen as they passed between the two Bays. Just lying off the prominent Cape about a half mile was Gull Island. This rocky island had taken many fishing schooners over the years. Five miles further north was the treacherous Harrys Grounds, a bank with many shoals, rising to only a few feet below the surface.

In April 1841, the House of Assembly passed "An Act to make provision for the establishment of a lighthouse on Cape Bonavista." The Lighthouse Board sent out their Secretary, a Mr. Ambrose Shea, to decide the best site for the new lighthouse. As a young man, he was the managing partner of Shea & Company, Newfoundland agents for the Allan Line of Royal Mail Steamships. The firm operated packet boats that plied between Liverpool, St. John's, and Boston, taking advantage of the influx of Irish in the first half of the nineteenth century. His expertise in maritime operations qualified him well to advise the Board on the selection of the best site for the new lighthouse. Ambrose Shea would go on to became a famous Newfoundland politician; he was elected as a Member of the House of Assembly only a few years later. A pro-Confederate, he represented the Newfoundland government in the talks in Charlottetown in 1864. In the 1880s, he became Prime Minister of Newfoundland, and eventually, Governor of Bahamas.

But in 1841, this young man stood high on the cliffs at Cape Bonavista on a sunny July day and considered the final site for the lighthouse. Cape L'Argent lay three and a half miles southeast of the Cape. It had a reputation of being frequently enveloped in fog so he turned his attention to Cape Bonavista.

A small, high island was actually the very tip of Cape Bonavista. This island was separated from the main headland by "a passage sufficiently wide to permit a punt to row through in fair weather." Shea reasoned, "A suspension bridge would be necessary for this purpose, and I doubt much even if the Commissioners felt disposed to sanction so large an expenditure as this would involve, whether the object to be gained would be commensurate." He recommended that the lighthouse should be built directly adjacent to this island, beside the one hundred and fifty foot high cliff.

The design was prepared by Trinity House in England that winter. It would be a building similar in many ways to the lighthouses at Cape Spear and Harbour Grace Island. Work was contracted to John Saunders, a local contractor, for £717. A thirty-foot square two-storey house was constructed. A stone tower rose through the centre of the building. The Scottish engineers strengthened the structure with sturdy 9" x 9" posts twice the diameter of regular construction. They included the architectural detail of the "false" windows used at Cape Spear. The work proceeded satisfactorily through the summer of 1842.

It was during this time that the Lighthouse Board began their search for a suitable light mechanism for the building. Contacting their consulting engineers, Robert Stevenson and Sons in Scotland, they learned that the mechanism at the famous Bell Rock was slated to be replaced the following year. This lighthouse was built by Stevenson thirty years before on a submerged reef known as Inchcape or Bell Rock, twelve miles off the east coast of Forfarshire in Scotland. The massive stone lighthouse was considered one of the great engineering wonders of the world.

The light mechanism itself consisted of sixteen Argand lamps illuminated with whale oil. The copper reflectors were made in Birmingham in 1811 and were arranged in an iron frame that rotated every ninety seconds, alternating white and red lights. The Commissioners described it as "the lighting apparatus (which) is of a very superior character - unequalled, the Board believe, by anything of the kind on this side of the Atlantic."

They sent Robert Oke, the keeper at Harbour Grace Island, to supervise the installation of the light mechanism. He had proven him-

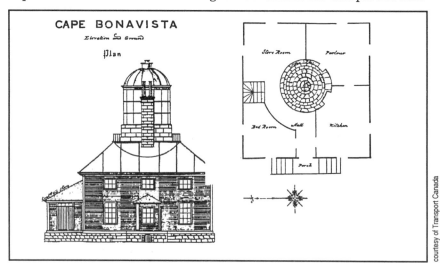

CAPE BONAVISTA

Elevation to ground

Plan

Store Room   Parlour

Bed Room   Hall   Kitchen

Porch

courtesy of Transport Canada

"*Engraving by Robert Oke showing Cape Bonavista Lighthouse in 1860.*"

"Cape Bonavista in the distance."

self as an excellent foreman during the construction of that lighthouse. When he arrived at Cape Bonavista with the English mechanism, he discovered that the contractor had done quite a bad job in constructing the stone tower. Oke insisted that it be rebuilt before he would install the light. This delayed the project into the winter of 1843. The delay so angered the members of the House of Assembly that the Lighthouse Board was taken to task over the delay during Spring Session of the Legislature. The tower was rebuilt in the summer, and the light was finally exhibited for the first time on September 11. It was built for a total cost of £3,024, substantially more that it cost to build Cape Spear.

The Lighthouse Board hired a fifty-year-old Irishman from Taghom, County Wexford to be the first keeper at Cape Bonavista. Jeremiah White had come over from Ireland as a young man of twenty-eight years during the height of the Irish immigration. After he was hired, White was sent to Cape Spear for three weeks apprenticing under Emanual Warre. The Lighthouse Board wanted him to learn the skills and tasks required of a keeper. He learned them well, for he remained as keeper for nearly thirty years. In 1857, his oldest son Nicholas became his assistant. Nicholas was groomed to take over the lighthouse when his father retired.

In 1871, at the ripe old age of seventy-nine years, Jeremiah finally relinquished the responsibility of the lighthouse to his son Nicholas. Nicholas would keep the light at Cape Bonavista for six only years; he died on New Years Eve, 1877, at the age of forty-two years. Similar to Cape Spear, the job of operating the lighthouse fell to the next youngest son, Matthew White. His younger brother Thomas became his assistant.

The first half of the 1880s would pass relatively uneventfully for the two brothers. The old light mechanism and the aging building would require constant attention to maintain them in the ferocious environment out at the Cape. In the spring of 1885, one storm in particular would be etched on their minds and the minds of everyone in Bonavista forever. The description of hurricane would hardly be appropriate, for it was said to be the worst in memory. It came from the east pushing a tremendous sea before it. It broke on the northeast coast of Newfoundland on June 5, just as the many schooners were preparing to depart for the Labrador fishery. That night, the hurricane struck with such force that all the wooden stages built around Bonavista harbour were flattened. As many as six unmanned schooners lying at anchor in the exposed bay were driven ashore.

One majestic barquentine had been moored out in Bonavista harbour that night. The huge square-rigged sailing ship *Christabel* was from Norway; she was heavily laden with supplies for the Labrador fishery. By six in the morning, the *Christabel* was in trouble, she was dragging her anchors, driven by the hurricane towards the jagged rocks at Canaille Point just south of the harbour. The term *canaille* is actually a French word which means *wicked* or *evil*. Captain Hendricks knew that they would be lost if they were to strike the evil reef. The only way the anchors would have a chance to withstand the force of the wind, would be to reduce the resistance caused by its four great masts. Captain Hendricks ordered his terrified crew to cut the rigging and let the masts fall like huge trees overboard. As the night fell, with the hurricane still raging, the disabled ship's anchors finally held only a ship's length from the jagged rocks. All those on board knew that if the chains would part during the night, then the ship would be smashed in minutes against the frightening shoal. The townsfolk built a great bonfire on shore to act as a beacon for the crew, should the anchors let go.

The storm continued unabated throughout the night and into the next day. At daybreak three men from Bonavista town volunteered to row a skiff out to the stricken vessel. They manoeuvered the boat into the lee side of the *Cristabell*, grasping on to a line thrown by the men on board. As the sea crashed just beyond the ship onto the rocks at Canaille Point, the crew transferred to the little boat. Fully loaded, they had to pick their way through the harbour that was strewn with the wreckage of the six wooden schooners. The barquentine managed to ride out the storm, having come within a breath of destruction. The bravery of the three local men was not forgotten. A monument commemorating their courage that stormy day was erected on "White Rock," the high hill overlooking the town. It remains there today.

Matthew White, like his older brother Nicholas, was not well during the latter years of his stewardship of the Cape Bonavista light. Inspector Nevill reported in 1888 that "Early in the new year, the keeper (Matthew), on the grounds of ill health, applied for and obtained permission to abstain from duty for a time, hoping that rest would be restorative. It did not have the desired effect, and it became necessary later in the season to make new arrangements for the discharge of duties of the

70

station. This has been done by appointing the assistant keeper (Thomas) to the sole keepership. The invalided keeper, a faithful officer for many years, has been provided with a retiring allowance." After taking charge of the station, Thomas White, the third brother, arranged for better accommodations to be constructed for his family. The original residence had suffered badly from the severe weather that buffeted the wooden lighthouse. A substantial two-storey, Victorian house was built next to the original building.

The old light mechanism that had served mariners for nearly eighty years was beginning to cause problems during the years after Thomas had become keeper. Inspector Nevill complained about the condition of the old mechanism in each of his annual reports between 1890 and 1895. "The machine operating the light is getting very much worn, and cannot

"Cape Bonavista lighthouse with new residence."

be relied on for any length of time. It has been used since 1810, having been installed at Bell Rock." In 1895, the Government finally agreed to replace it. They solved the problem in a typically Newfoundland way— they replaced the old Scottish mechanism with another old Scottish mechanism. Amazingly, though, this one stood the test of one hundred and seventy-five years. Nine great copper parabolic reflectors complete with the kerosene lamps with their tall glass chimneys were installed in an iron frame. The mechanism first cast its light from a lighthouse on the Isle of May off the Scottish coast. In 1847, it was sold to the Newfoundland Lighthouse Board and was installed at Cape Pine a few years later. In 1869, the light mechanism was relocated to Harbour Grace Island where it remained until 1894. The following year, it made its last move to Cape Bonavista. This light mechanism is still there.

In September 1895, fifty-seven year old Thomas White, the third and last son of Jeremiah White, died after being keeper for only seven years. Inspector White reported to the House of Assembly, "By his death, the service lost one of its most efficient and trustworthy staff."

Thomas's son, Fred, became the last of the White family to operate the lighthouse at Cape Bonavista. He took over, with his father's death, at the young age of twenty-one years. For the next fifteen years he kept the light; his assistant was Sam Mifflin.

It was during this time that another heroic rescue took place down on the rocks at Canaille Point in Bonavista harbour. Ironically, it was another Norwegian ship that was involved. Ryan and Company were in those days operating a merchant trade between Bonavista and Europe. They were exporting the products of the cod and seal fishery, importing the general supplies and provisions necessary for the residents of this large Newfoundland community.

In the fall of 1907, they had consigned a great white clipper ship *Snorre* with the bulk of their winter supplies. On September 18, the brand new ship arrived off Cape Bonavista, her graceful bow cutting easily through the sea swells that were building in advance of a fall storm. She moored safely in the harbour off the Ryan and Company wharf for the night, with sturdy anchors placed off her bow and stern. Most of the crew went ashore to enjoy a home-cooked meal. Five men remained on board to watch the ship.

During the evening, the storm worsened into a raging gale. The exposed harbour provided no protection from the enormous sea that was sweeping in across Moses Point on the north side of the harbour. The stress was too great for the anchor chains to bear. At midnight, first one, then the other, parted. The *Snorre* was cast free and drifted downwind towards the doom of Canaille Point. At midnight distress flares were fired from the stricken ship, awaking the townsfolk of Bonavista. They watched in horror as the *Snorre* crashed into the rocks stern first. The five crew climbed the rigging as huge twenty-five-foot waves broke over the ship. A group of fishermen, led by thirty-seven year old Louis Little, organized a rescue; they formed a human chain out into the surf. In the blackness of the night, with the wind howling around them, these courageous men made repeated attempts to get a line aboard. As one of the crew attempted to swim ashore, he was crushed by the waves against the jagged reef. Finally, they succeeded in their task and, drawing the

72

line tight, the remainder of the crew began to make the arduous transfer to shore. They drew themselves along the line, hand over hand, as the seas pounded and buffeted them. One man lost his grip and fell into the sea. Lewis Little, at great risk to his own life, entered the water and saved the man. Several other rescuers narrowly missed being washed away as they attempted to reach the ship. As the last man reached shore, a huge wave struck the beautiful white ship and she broke in two with her tall masts toppling into the surf. Within an hour there was nothing left of that great Norwegian Clipper ship. These humble Bonavista men were honoured as heros in Newfoundland by the Carnegie Foundation. In Norway, King Haarkon decorated them for their acts of bravery in saving his countrymen.

In 1913, the Lighthouse Department began construction of a fog alarm on Cape Island. This is the small high rocky island located just beside the lighthouse. They built a rather rickety wooden foot bridge to connect the fog alarm building with the lighthouse station. A young man, Hubert Abbott, was hired to operate the fog alarm; he lived in a small house built on the island. Abbott married and began to raise a family on the tenuous site. In 1919, another terrific storm struck the northeastern coast of Newfoundland. The seas swept over the 150-foot-high island, carrying away Abbott's house and the bridge with it. Apparently, Abbott and his family managed to escape with little more than their lives.

In 1923, he took over the operation of the lighthouse and the new fog alarm. The Victorian two-storey house that had been built for Thomas White in 1888 was demolished because it hadn't withstood the severe weather conditions at the Cape. A modest bungalow was built in its place; that was where Hubert Abbott and his large family lived for many years of service. He retired in 1960 after an amazing forty-seven years. Several men have kept the light since then including Clyde Purchase, John Hyde and most recently Norm Howdsell.

In 1966, the Department of Transportation decided to replace the old lighthouse. They built a very functional but rather unromantic steel tower just beside the original building. Realizing the historic significance of the lighthouse, the Federal Department signed it over to the Provincial Government after over one and a quarter centuries of ceaseless operation. During the late 1970s, the Historic Resources Division of the Newfoundland government restored the building to the 1870s when Jeremiah White operated the lighthouse with his son Nicholas. Staff with the Division, wearing costumes typical of that time, act as guides to this beautiful building on this breathtaking site.

The drive from St. John's to Cape Bonavista takes about three and a half hours. Heading west on the Trans Canada Highway, travel about 200 km to Clarenville, and turn north onto the Discovery Trail (Route 230). This highway takes you out along the Bonavista Peninsula, through rolling hills with mature stands of spruce and birch. The landscape gradually gives way to more stunted vegetation and shallow rock-rimmed ponds and gullies. You will pass through towns such as Port Union and Catalina, very historic in their own right. It is about 120 km from Clarenville to the approaches to Bonavista Town. The Discovery Trail passes through the centre of the community, meeting Route 235.

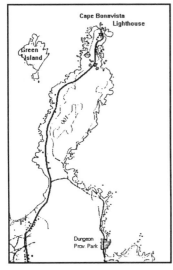

This roadway will take you out to the Cape. Turn right at the intersection, past the Town Hall, and travel northward out of Bonavista on Route 235.

As the last few multi-coloured houses slip away, you will become aware that you are headed out the narrow point of the peninsula. On your immediate left is the coastline of Bonavista Bay. Just offshore, you should notice a low island, the top of which is completely covered in long green grass. This is Green Island that housed the wooden fort during the troubled times of the early eighteenth century. It was to this windswept island that George Skiffington led the terrorized inhabitants of Bonavista in 1705. On your right are the low barrens and boggy meadows of Cape Bonavista. These meadows have been used by the community for grazing their cattle and sheep for nearly three hundred years. Beyond these barrens lies Trinity Bay.

At about six kilometres from the Town Hall, you should make the final drive up to the lighthouse parking lot. You should notice just off to the left a modest monument commemorating the discovery of the New World by John Cabot.

The climb up the hill to the lighthouse affords a spectacular view of the two bays separated by the finger-like Bonavista Peninsula. On a clear day, you can make out the jagged sea stacks known as Spillar's Point, and beyond, lining up with this point, is Cape L'Argent. This was the alternate site for the lighthouse that Ambrose Shea had considered so many years ago. The red and white striped lighthouse is built on a high rocky pinnacle beside a sheer rock cliff that drops one hundred and fifty feet straight into the sea. A narrow channel separates Cape Island from the mainland. In the canyon between Cape Island and the cliff, black guillemots and puffins soar. These little sea birds are searching for small fish for their offspring safely hidden on the Island.

Climb up the stone staircase built inside the ancient lighthouse tower and stand protected in the lantern room. Look eastward toward the horizon where John Cabot's ship rode five hundred years before.

Cape Pine
(Flash .2 seconds; eclipse 4.8 seconds)
The Imperial Lighthouse

"A better opportunity I could not have had of viewing this really terrific headland, as I ran close round it at the back of the breakers, opening out point after point. The mountainous sea left by the recent gale was breaking in sheets of foam upon its sharp pointed rocks, and sending the white spray fifty to sixty feet up its high and inaccessible cliffs of dark grey clay-slate. Lit up by the last rays of the setting sun, 'twas a scene to be remembered, magnificently beautiful ..."
from Captain Henry Bayfield's Journal, August 1847

Captain Henry Bayfield was a young Naval surveyor who had the responsibility of surveying much of the Gulf of St. Lawrence in the late 1840s. In the summer of 1847 he was asked by the British Admiralty to undertake a survey of Trepassey Bay on the south coast of the Avalon Peninsula. That spring, Trinity House had recommended to the British House of Commons that "the measure of lighting the south-eastern part of Newfoundland would be effectually accomplished by the erection of a Lighthouse on Cape Pine, on the south-eastern most extremity of that land, ... likewise that all vessels bound to or from ports or places situate between St. John's and Cape Cod, including the River St. Lawrence, would be benefited by the establishment of (a) lighthouse in the above mentioned situation... "

The Admiralty had become increasingly concerned with the loss of shipping and lives along the coastline near Cape Pine. This high headland marks the very southern tip of the Avalon Peninsula, and forms the eastern point of St. Mary's Bay. The large, exposed bay was well known by fishermen and mariners for its dense sea fogs and rich fishery. In prevailing southerly and southeasterly winds, terrifically strong currents set into St. Mary's Bay. Inspector White would write years later:

> "Fishermen on the coast have informed me that the strength of the in-setting current is at times such as to force trap buoys - twenty gallon casks - under water. It is under such conditions of the current that ships are drawn bodily, so to speak, in on the coast, although the correct course to clear the land has been carefully shaped and vigilantly steered. It may with reason be assumed that every ship lost in this locality was at the time of striking supposed by its navigator to be several miles seaward of Cape Pine."

For years, the British Admiralty had been losing ships on the coastline near this spectacular headland. In the fall of 1816, two warships were lost at nearby St. Shott's. The HMS *Comus*, a five hundred ton frigate, was followed by HMS *Harpooner* a month later. In the case of the *Harpooner*, there was an enormous loss of life. The aging troop carrier went aground in a dense fog near Cape Pine. She was loaded with British marines and their families who were returning to Britain after the end of the War of 1812. Over three hundred and fifty people died in the disaster, making it one of the worst accidents in Newfoundland marine history. Six years later, a third warship, the HMS *Drake* was wrecked with a loss of another thirteen men.

Through the 1820s and 1830s, more ships were lost. Most of these were eastward bound from Canadian and American ports. They were making for the headlands of the Southern Avalon. From there, the mariners intended to turn their ships east for Europe.

Just as the British Admiralty had particular interest in this deadly cape, it was not overlooked by the Newfoundland Lighthouse Commissioners either. In their report to the House of Assembly in 1841, they wrote:

> "With this view, we would submit to your Excellency, that the mischiefs arising from the want of a Light on Cape Pine, before so acknowledged, have been rendered more apparent by the events of the past year, for seldom before were the losses of life and property in that vicinity so great within any equal time. That a recurrence of such events may be mainly prevented by the establishment of a light, few will, for a moment, be inclined to doubt."

Throughout the 1840s, the House of Assembly continued to make similar requests to the British House of Commons for assistance in building a lighthouse at Cape Pine. Years before, the British Admiralty had provided a grant to the Nova Scotian government to build the lighthouse on Sambro Island at the outer entrance to Halifax harbour. In May 1847, the British Parliament finally agreed to provide a grant worth £2000 for the construction of the Cape Pine Lighthouse, "subject to the condition that provision shall be made by the Legislature of Newfoundland...for the future maintenance of the light."

They also suggested that the other British North American Provinces should help Newfoundland in the operation of the new lighthouse. When these provinces politely declined the offer, the Lighthouse Commissioners were quite insulted. "The Board cannot here forebear to express their surprise, that the other (BNA) Colonies should persist in the injustice of refusing any aid for the support of the Light at Cape Pine, from which they will derive the chief advantage. The whole charge for its maintenance is a most unfair tax on the funds of this Colony."

The Admiralty commissioned Alexander Gordon, a consulting engineer in London, to design and cast a pre-fabricated lighthouse for Cape Pine. He had developed a system of interlocking cast iron plates which, when assembled, would provide an effective, economical approach to the problem of building lighthouses on inaccessible sites. This approach had been successfully used in Britain since 1803. It would be the first of many such examples to be built in Newfoundland. The Lighthouse Board had experimented with stone, brick and wooden lighthouses over the years. Not one of these approaches would have a lasting effect on lighthouse construction in Newfoundland. During the 1880s and 1890s, there was a veritable boom of Newfoundland lighthouse construction. It was during this time that many cast iron lighthouses were built using the techniques developed by Alexander Gordon. At the beginning of the twentieth century, reinforced concrete became the preferred construction material.

In 1847, Captain Bayfield selected a magnificent headland overlooking Trepassey Bay. The lighthouse would be located on the highest point of land at the very edge of a 315-foot black slate cliff. The lands to the west of Cape Pine were considerably lower. Ships approaching from the west passing St. Mary's Bay would see the new light at Cape Pine just as easily as those to the northeast.

Alexander Gordon did a superb job in designing the Cape Pine Lighthouse. It would be a beautifully proportioned, gracefully tapered fifty-foot iron tower. A wide, finely detailed iron gallery was designed to encircle the large lantern structure at the top.

Construction began on this inaccessible site in 1849. The curved iron sections had to be landed by boat in Arnold Cove. This is an exposed cove that lies between Cape Pine and Cape Freels just to the west. The crates were hoisted up the cliff and carted over to the construction site. The English crew lifted the sections into place and bolted them together using three-inch iron bolts.

A used light mechanism was purchased from the Northern Lighthouse Board. It had operated on the Isle of May off the coast of Scotland for nearly forty years. The mechanism was installed atop the tower during the summer of 1850; the light was first exhibited on New Year's Day, 1851. This same revolving light eventually ended up at Cape Bonavista, forty-five years later.

As beautiful as the building exterior was, there were real problems with the interior of the lighthouse. Gordon had been familiar with the temperate climate of Great Britain; he intended the keeper, his family and the assistant to live inside the lighthouse on the lower floors of the structure. He designed the lighthouse to be extra wide - a full nineteen feet in diameter, with the two lower floors finished as a residence. The two floors were connected by an intricate circular stair. Unfortunately, Gordon did not give careful consideration to how the lighthouse could be heated.

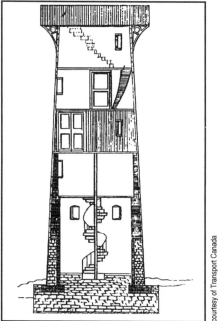

"Section through Cape Pine Lighthouse"

Henry Hearder, an Englishman, had been appointed as the first keeper at Cape Pine. He moved his wife and five children into the lighthouse in the fall of 1850 when the British government officially handed the station over to the Colonial government. Hearder realized in the first winter that the lighthouse was quite uninhabitable.

By February Hearder was compelled to write the Lighthouse Commissioners to complain about the miserable situation at Cape Pine.

"GENTLEMEN, I beg leave to lay before you a statement of the Tower as a place of residence, for which it is by no means adapted. Judge of our situation when we cannot keep the Tower or porch doors shut with the fires in. Up to the present, the doors have not been shut during the winter, with the winds from NNE to SSE. We are kept in constant agitation with our fires and are sometimes obliged to put them out altogether. The smoke is very injurious to the reflectors and lamps and causes a great deal of trouble. In gales of wind, the draft running up the spiral stairs, thence to the light room,

78

causes much trouble and difficulty in keeping the machine to revolve in proper time, and this can only be remedied by keeping the doors closed, which obliges us to put out the fires, and makes it truly miserable for us to live at this inclement season. However, I am happy to say the lights have steadily gone correct during the winter.

"The joints in the Tower in several places are leaky as are also the windows. The quantities of water come rushing in all directions; we have not had a dry bed since our arrival here. From our exposed and elevated position, the rain finds its way through every crevice - Nothing but a dwelling attached to the Tower can possibly do here; for in common gales we cannot venture out on the cliff without risk of being blown over, there being no safety fence at the cliff side."

Hearder finally moved his family into a small shed that had been built adjacent to the lighthouse for the construction engineer. During the summer of 1851, a substantial residence was built just to the rear of the lighthouse. The house was connected to the lighthouse by an enclosed walkway.

Arnold Cove was very exposed; landing supplies was difficult and often dangerous. That summer, a thirteen-mile road was built between Cape Pine and Trepassey at a cost of £788. In the years to follow, the residents of St. Shott's would use it to visit Trepassey. This irked the Lighthouse Board because they were charged with the expensive repairs and upkeep of the road.

The light mechanism was initially operated as a revolving light flashing once every twenty seconds. Inspector Oke, wishing to reduce the wear on the mechanism, quickly ordered it slowed to flash every thirty seconds. Five years later, Cape Race was built across Trepassey Bay. Cape Race quickly became recognized as a landfall light for shipping bound for North American ports from Europe. In 1864, Inspector Oke realized the importance of having a more distinctive light there so he recommended that the Cape Pine light be fixed and Cape Race to revolve.

In September 1866, George Hewitt became the lighthouse keeper at Cape Pine replacing Henry Hearder who had died earlier that year. Hewitt had been born in Ireland and had been assistant keeper at nearby Cape Race since 1858. He brought with him an Irish wife and a one-year-old son, George. So began a one-hundred-year dynasty lasting four generations where the Hewitt family would be responsible for the operation of the Cape Pine lighthouse.

The years passed slowly at Cape Pine. The lives of Hewitt and his family would be regulated by the operation of the lighthouse and the passing of seasons. Tortuous dark winters would give way to those glorious sunny days of summer on that grassy summit. Hewitt's oldest daughter, Sarah, had been born at Cape Pine shortly after her father became the keeper there. As she grew older and more children were born at Cape Pine, Sarah had the responsibility of tending the large garden dug just behind the lighthouse. The produce added a bit of variety to the meagre provisions provided by the Lighthouse Service.

When her chores were done, Sarah would often sit with the younger children perched on the steep grassy banks below the lighthouse. There they would watch the antics of the little Atlantic puffins *(Fratercula artica)* that nested there each summer. These comical little birds can be easily distinguished from the other sea birds by their large parrot-like red bills. Each spring, after spending the winter far offshore,

Atlantic Puffin; Adults in summer.

courtesy of Ian L. Jones

hundreds of these birds would return to the grassy banks of Cape Pine. The turf banks were ideal for digging burrows which served as nests for a single, dull white egg. Their distinctive black and white plumage stood out in the lush, green grass. The puffins were excellent swimmers and spent the summer fishing for caplin and other small fish off the cliffs of Cape Pine.

Hewitt and his eldest son, George, frequently travelled out onto the barrens above the Cape to take a caribou to supplement their diet. These were the large Woodland Caribou *(Rangifer tarandus)* that are native to Newfoundland. After calving near the Samonier River in the Central Avalon, several thousand animals travelling in small family groups migrate to the open coastal barrens of the Southern Avalon. They journeyed to these treeless headlands to escape the swarms of mosquitoes inland and to feed on the lush summer vegetation that grew on the barrens. A large stag with his dark brown coat, flowing white mane and large rack of antlers, weighed as much as 600 pounds and stood as high as 50 inches. Such a male would typically guard over a harem of a dozen doe and offspring. The doe were smaller and lighter in color. It was an impressive sight when Hewitt would scan the barrens each June and see literally hundreds of animals feeding on the headland at Cape Pine.

In the 1880s and 1890s, many ships were lost on the eleven mile stretch of coastline between Cape Pine west past St. Shott's to Cape English in St. Mary's Bay. The majority of these steamers were eastward bound for Europe.

Fort Amherst Lighthouse at South Head

Cape Spear Lighthouse

James Cantwell's kitchen

Cape Bonavista Lighthouse

Catoptric light mechanism - Cape Bonavista

Cape Pine Lighthouse

Woodland caribou crossing the road near Cape Pine

Point Amour Lighthouse

Entrance way at Point Amour

Cape Race Lighthouse

Cape Race Lighthouse at sunrise

Ferryland Head Lighthouse

Tom Ryan and the light mechanism at Cape Race

The original lighthouse from Cape Race now in Ottawa

Cape St. Mary's Lighthouse

Gannets at Bird Rock

Cape Norman Lighthouse

Cypripedium Calceolus, orchid growing at Cape Norman

Ferryland Head Lighthouse

Cape Ray Lighthouse

1882 was a particularly bad year. In the period of two months, three large ships were lost near Cape Pine. The new steamship *Gertrude*, owned by the English trading company of Gordon and Stamp, had departed in mid-May from New Orleans. She was bound for Copenhagen with a load of maize corn. The Captain had stopped in Sydney to replenish the ship's coal bunkers before he headed her east for Cape Race and beyond to Denmark. By June 4, the *Gertrude* was passing along the south coast of Newfoundland leaving the Burin Peninsula and Placentia Bay to her port side. The south coast of the Avalon Peninsula was completely enveloped in a dense fog. The officers on watch were forced to navigate using dead reckoning, intending to give the treacherous coastline a wide berth. While a gale had passed through the area the day before, the winds had calmed. As evening darkness settled on the steamship that foggy night, all seemed well. Suddenly, dead ahead, a three hundred foot perpendicular cliff appeared out of the mist and before they could slow her progress, the *Gertrude* drove hard and high up on a rock ledge at its base.

They had grounded near Western Head just southwest of Cape Pine. The *Gertrude* hung on the ledge with her bottom torn out. Her fate was sealed; the ship was a complete wreck. While a heavy surf pounded the ship, the light winds meant that the ship would not break up immediately.

The twenty-two crew transferred into three lifeboats and when the fog lifted the next morning, they were picked up by a fishing schooner passing through the area. Within weeks the *Gertrude* would slip off the ledge and sink in deeper water but not before the brigantine *Eagle* would be lost near the same spot. On August 13, in a heavy sea, the 1,650 ton steamship *Action* bound from Montreal with a cargo of wood broke up at Western Head just as the previous ships had.

While there was no loss of life in each of these incidents, clearly the lighthouse at Cape Pine was not effective during the frequent periods of sea fog. In an editorial in the St. John's daily *Evening Telegram* three days after this last wreck, the public's concern over the situation was expressed.

"Some two years ago, the eastern and western heads of St. Shott's were investigated by Mr. Nevill as to which head was most suitable for a fog alarm and I believe the western head was decided upon. But since that time nothing has been heard about it and St. Shott's and neighbourhood have picked up nine steamers and some sailing vessels; but it is not for the people of that place to condemn, as it is to their benefit that no fog alarm be placed there. However, the next steamer's crew may not fare as well. All hands may find a watery grave, and then it will be too late for a fog alarm."

Actually, Inspector Nevill had recommended a fog alarm to be built at Cape Freels just to the west of Cape Pine. "Such a signal would go far to prevent the many losses caused by the strong currents that set with peculiar force into the Bay while fog prevails - currents that carry vessels out of their course to almost certain destruction." It would take nearly thirty more years before a fog alarm would finally be constructed at Cape Freels.

Sarah Hewitt died of diphtheria in the fall of 1889; she was only twenty-one years old. She was buried on a low hill overlooking the lighthouse station; her grave marked with a white stone. George Hewitt died at Cape Pine after being the keeper there for forty-four years. His oldest son, George J. Hewitt, took over the responsibility of maintaining the light in 1910.

"*George Hewitt and family, 1920.*"

In 1912, a marine tragedy was to take place that would finally cause a fog alarm to be built at Cape Pine. It was a wild night in December, when the SS *Florence*, a graceful 2,500 ton steamer, began her final leg on a trip from Halifax. On board the Furness Liner were twenty-seven passengers and crew bound for St. John's for the Christmas holidays. During the evening of December 19, she was gripped in a powerful storm on the south coast of Newfoundland. The storm varied between blinding snow squalls and freezing rain. The *Florence* was making slow headway in the heavy gale, struggling in the huge sea. She struck at 3:30 in the morning at Marine's Cove, just west of St. Shott's. Marine's Cove was named for the British Marines who drowned as the result of the wreck of the HMS *Harpooner*, lost there nearly one hundred years before. The *Florence* had struck with such force that she was driven across the reef to stop against the base of a precipitous cliff. Her graceful Clipper bow hung over the smooth, black slate ledge. In the darkness of the night,

"Cape Pine Lighthouse, 1920."

all twenty-seven souls climbed over the bowsprit to drop and huddle for a time on the exposed ledge. It was clear to all that the cliff face could not be scaled. So, at daybreak, they returned to the ship to await the end of the storm. But their respite on board the *Florence* was not much better for the ship had begun to break up in the heavy sea. At 11 am, Captain Barr allowed five men to make an attempt to go for help. The five men rowed a small boat to a cove nearby. From there they managed to climb the cliff. At nightfall on the heights above the shipwreck, they discovered an abandoned fisherman's shed. That is where they spent the night as the gale raged around them. The next morning, nothing remained of the *Florence* except splintered wood thrown high by the waves. All of the twenty-two people who had remained on board the doomed ship had perished in the night. The five survivors walked back along the headland to reach to St. Shott's that evening. News of the fate of the Florence rocked St. John's and Halifax.

Within two years a fog alarm was built at the very tip of Cape Freels by the Canadian Government. Fog alarms were built at several other Canadian stations including Point Amour and Cape Race around the same time. Michael Myrick with his wife and four children came over from Cape Race to operate the fog alarm. The fog alarm at Cape Freels was connected to the light station by a short twenty minute walk across the barrens.

It was Myrick who watched from the cliffs below the fog alarm as another marine disaster took place on a reef just offshore. Ironically, it would be a case of mistaken identity that would cause the accident. In

May 1923, the magnificent, eleven thousand ton liner SS*Marvale*, owned by the Canadian Pacific Railway, went aground in dense fog on a voyage from Montreal to Glasgow. There were 236 passengers on board, consisting mostly of English and Scottish citizens. Also on board was a huge cargo of canned meats, cheese and flour. Apparently, the Captain, upon hearing what he thought was the fog signal from Cape Race, altered course straight into the reef at Cape Freels. At 3:50 pm, the *Marvale* struck going full out at thirteen knots. She drove high up on the reef. Luckily, the sea was dead calm. Captain Lewis realized that his beautiful ship was a complete wreck; he ordered the *Marvale* abandoned. Amazingly, all passengers and crew transferred safely to lifeboats. The survivors rowed for St. Shott's making it by nightfall. Dozens of boats from St. Shott's and Trepassey descended on the *Marvale* in days to come to reap her spoils. Many parts of Newfoundland had been impoverished by the depression in the salt fish trade. The cargo of food was a godsend for many outport communities along this shore.

In 1930, the fog alarm was moved to a site just below the Cape Pine Lighthouse, beside the puffin colony. James Myrick operated the fog alarm having taken over from his father. A modern fog alarm still exists there today.

During the mid-1930s George J. Hewitt was replaced by his son George T. Hewitt. George T. Hewitt retired in 1946. His younger brother Val (Valentine) Hewitt took over from him. Michael Myrick worked as his assistant. Val Hewitt retired in 1973 and Michael Myrick took over as the head keeper at Cape Pine. Today Tom Finlay operates the lighthouse; Peter Myrick is the assistant keeper.

It takes a bit more than about two hours to drive to Cape Pine from St. John's, travelling along the Southern Shore Highway (Route 10). You will pass the turn for Ferryland Head Lighthouse and later the road for Cape Race.

About 170 km from St. John's, after driving through Trepassey, you should watch for a left hand turnoff for the community of St. Shott's. A dirt road bears off to the left only three kilometres after making that initial turn from Route 10. The last eight or nine kilometres straight across the barrens is quite easy going. The Department of Transportation maintains this gravel road in good condition. If you travel to Cape Pine in the late spring and early summer, you will see herds of woodland caribou that roam these barrens. The series of headlands between Trepassey and St. Peter's still support a large herd of several thousand animals. On a clear day, you are sure to see several small herds leisurely feeding on the caribou moss that is common over much of this barren landscape. These majestic animals have rather poor eyesight so it is fairly easy to approach them downwind. Their keen sense of hearing and smell may prevent you from getting too close before their big crescent-shaped hoofs carry them back out across the barrens.

As you approach the coast, you will see the outline of the Cape Pine Lighthouse silhouetted on the horizon. The fifty-foot iron tower with its contrasting red and white horizontal bands remains almost exactly as it was built by Alexander Gordon over one hundred and forty years

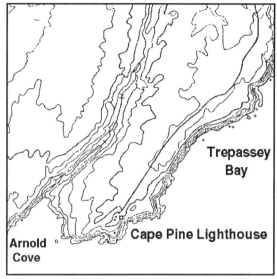

ago. In recognition of the history of this place, the building was identified as a Federal Heritage structure in 1989. The original keeper's residence that was built for Henry Hearder was demolished in the 1950s. Two modern single storey residences for the keeper and his assistant were built in its place and are still located nearby.

Ask the keeper on duty to take you inside the iron structure. The original circular stair winds up through this high space, brightly lit by a series of small square windows located above. It was here that Henry Hearder brought his family in 1850. It is hard to imagine the misery that they experienced that first winter so many years ago. As you pass through the storeroom located just below the lantern room, notice the iron ventilation pipes that run along the ceiling. These were vent pipes that supplied air necessary for combustion of the seal oil or kerosene fuel. The actual lantern room is a bit of a disappointment. The massive light mechanism has been replaced by a minuscule 500 watt light bulb. The light is projected by two small bullseye lenses. It is hard to believe that this simple system exhibits a light having a strength of 130,000 candle power, equal to most of the Victorian lights.

While the vacancy of the old lantern room is disappointing, the long climb up the stairs is worthwhile. The view from the top of Cape Pine Lighthouse is spectacular. From here you can look eastward across the magnificent Trepassey Bay. The faint headland thirty kilometres distant is Mistaken Point; just beyond lies Cape Race. Look just a kilometre west from your vantage point to jagged Cape Freels. It was here that the first fog alarm was built in 1914, and it was here that the SS *Marvale* met her fate in 1923.

Walk down to the present location of the fog alarm building, just east of here along the coastline you can still find the colony of Atlantic Puffins. It is one of the few Puffin colonies in Newfoundland that can be reached by car. Most colonies can be accessed only by boat. **You should stay on the dirt road that leads to the fog alarm. Beyond, the slope is steep and the grass is very slippery. One missed step might cause a deadly fall down the black slate rock cliff**. Rest for a while beside the fog alarm and look out across Trepassey Bay as Sarah and her brothers did so many years ago.

Point Amour
(Flash 16 seconds; eclipse 4 seconds)
The Straits Light

"Stones and rocks, frightful and rough...for in all the coasts of the north I did not see a cartload of earth. I believe that this is the land that God gave to Cain."

from Jacques Cartier's Journal, 1534

Newfoundland is separated from Labrador by the Strait of Belle Isle. This narrow body of water divides two important geological formations. The ancient Canadian Shield runs from the southeastern coast of Labrador westward through Quebec to Northern Ontario. It is one of the oldest geological formations in the world, some rocks are over one billion years old. Just across the Strait, the more recent Long Range Mountains run like a great rock spine down the west coast of Newfoundland. They are the start of the Appalachian Mountain Range that extends on through to the northeastern United States. The earlier geological formation forms the base for younger sedimentary rocks of the Long Range Mountains.

Much more recently, the "Straits" area between Newfoundland and Labrador received a series of glaciations. The unimaginable force exerted by these glaciers was sufficient to sink the land mass below the level of the sea. The most recent glaciation period reached its peak some

11,000 years ago. As the glaciers began to melt, these sunken areas rebounded forming new beaches and river deltas. Later, these coastal lowlands rose further, eventually becoming elevated well above sea level. Their remains can still be seen today as you travel on either side of the Strait of Belle Isle.

With the departure of the glaciers, the south coast of Labrador was visited by man. As early as 7000 BC, a race of aboriginal people settled there. It is believed that the *Maritime Archaic people* originally came from New England travelling northward across the mouth of the St. Lawrence River. They were searching for the large herds of harp seals which give birth to their young on the pan ice in the Gulf each spring. During the winter months, the Maritime Archaic Indians established small hunting camps in the many protected bays and wide, sandy beaches that exist on the south coast of Labrador. Following the spring seal hunt, the bands would break their camps to turn inland to pursue the large herds of woodland caribou. They also fished for the plentiful trout, salmon and arctic char that teemed in the icy rivers. Their people were to spread all along the Strait of Belle Isle area. Eventually they migrated across the Strait and established camps on the northwestern and northeastern coasts of Newfoundland as well. Their society ulti-mately gave way to an early Inuit civilization. These people migrated from Dorset Island far to the north of Labrador during the last five centuries BC. They lived a similar life as the Maritime Archaic people before them. The Dorset Eskimo people may have survived to the time of the early visits by the Vikings in 1000 AD before they finally disap-peared forever.

Five hundred years later, the Strait of Belle Isle was recognized by early European explorers as a great northern gateway from the Atlantic Ocean into the Gulf of St. Lawrence. In the spring of 1534, after first sighting land at Cape Bonavista, Jacques Cartier travelled northward and passed through the Strait of Belle Isle. He rested his weary men on one of the sandy bays of the south coast of Labrador before taking them southward again along the west coast of Newfoundland. In his Journal Cartier expressed his dismay at the stark landscape that he and his men witnessed…"stones and rocks, frightful and rough…for in all the coasts of the north I did not see a cartload of earth. I believe that this is the land that God gave to Cain." Cartier returned home to France but visited the Strait of Belle Isle again on his second trip the following year. He went on to explore the Gulf of St. Lawrence and established French outposts at Montreal and Quebec City.

Word of the plentiful resources that could be had along this coastline spread quickly. In the decades that followed Cartier's exploration, Europeans travelled to the Strait to establish summer fishing and whaling stations in many of the protected bays. Some were Basques from the mountainous region which is part of France and Spain. These hearty fishermen ventured out from their land bases on the south coast of Labrador in small boats to hunt for whales. After successfully killing these great mammals, they towed them back to their outposts for processing. At high tide the whalers would drag the carcasses up high on the beaches and begin to cut the thick layers of fat away from the body. This blubber was tossed into large copper pots set in a stone structure known as a *trywork*. Large fires were maintained beneath these kettles, fuelled by a constant supply of spruce logs. Later, the rendered oil was poured into wooden barrels for shipment back to Europe each fall. The Basques carried out this lucrative activity for fifty years on the south coast of Labrador until they abandoned the industry around 1600.

Throughout the seventeenth and most of the eighteenth centuries, French and English fishermen pursued the cod fishery on the excellent fishing grounds in the Strait of Belle Isle. After the Treaty of Paris in 1763, the French were effectively banished from North America. Similar to the northeastern coast of Newfoundland, the West Country fishermen and merchants were freed from the harassment by the French. They established a year round fishing station at English Point in Forteau Bay. This wide, sandy bay provided an excellent anchorage for ships riding out a winter storm. It was located at the head of fertile river estuary. The Forteau River, full of salmon, provided ready access inland for fur trapping and logging. The wealth of these resources proved to be a great magnet, attracting not just the English but the Americans and fishermen from Quebec.

Newfoundlanders also began travelling to southern Labrador in the summer to take part in what would become known as the "floater and stationer fishery." The floater fishermen stayed on board their boats throughout the summer season following the schools of northern cod as they migrated up the coast. The codfish were salted on board and dried when they returned home in the fall. The stationer fishermen departed from Conception, Trinity and Bonavista Bays in great schooner fleets each spring bound for countless land stations that were scattered along the southeast coast of Labrador. As the century drew to a close, hundreds of ships made spring trips to harbours such as Forteau and Battle Harbour to pursue the summer fishery. In 1809, the British Parliament transferred ownership of the coast of Labrador to the Newfoundland Colonial government.

The comings and goings of schooners during the summer fishing season were not the only activity that took place in the narrow strait. The most direct route between Europe and Canadian ports on the St. Lawrence River passed through the perilous Strait of Belle Isle. The Strait was known for its strong currents, dense sea fogs, shifting winds and errant icebergs. Completely blocked for six months each year with impenetrable pack ice, the northern route around Newfoundland was too difficult to be attempted by most sailing captains. They opted for the longer but much safer southern route around the south coast of Newfoundland. The Cabot Strait was much wider. Except for St. Paul's Island off Cape Breton, the route proved easier to negotiate in a sailing ship.

By the early nineteenth century, with the coming of steam power, more and more ships began attempting the northern entrance to the Gulf of St. Lawrence during the summer months. It was considered by the Province of Canada to be "the Gateway to the Continent." By 1850, both the British Admiralty and Trinity House in Quebec recognized the need for a series of major coastal lighthouses marking the northern route through to the Gulf of St. Lawrence. Four new lighthouses were ordered; they included one on Belle Isle that marked the very eastern entrance of the Strait. Another lighthouse was to be built on the west point of Anticosti Island, marking the western entrance. A third lighthouse was to be built at Cap des Rosier, on the North Shore of the St. Lawrence. The final one was to be built on a barren point of land on the eastern side of Forteau Bay. Known locally as Point Amour, it was just two miles east of English Point where the West Country men had settled a century before.

The lighthouse at Point Amour had the distinction of being the first of many lighthouses to be built within the jurisdiction of the Newfoundland government but owned and operated by the Canadian government. The Canadians took it upon themselves to construct several of the most important lighthouse stations on the Island in later years. While the Federal Ministry was always careful to obtain written permission from the government in St. John's, there was a certain amount of friction between them and the Newfoundland Lighthouse Service.

The Canadian Board of Works prepared the design for this stone lighthouse based on the experience of the Northern Lighthouse Board in Scotland. Robert Stevenson and others had developed the design of stone lighthouse structures to a high science. In the fall of 1853, the contract was let to François Baby. Monsieur Baby was an experienced contractor from Quebec. He was given the difficult task of constructing one of the tallest lighthouses in Canada on one of its most inaccessible sites. The lighthouse was to be built of limestone from quarries at Forteau Point and L'Anse-au-Loup. All other building materials had to be shipped in from Canada. Even the wood timbers had to be shipped since only stunted spruce could be had along this exposed shore. Most of the building materials were landed at the protected harbour at L'Anse-au-Loup and carted to the site at Point Amour.

The lighthouse was located on a fifty-five foot high grassy ridge that runs parallel to the jagged limestone coastline. It would take the contractor nearly four years to build it. Twenty-five feet wide at its base, the lighthouse rose gracefully one hundred and nine feet to the light and another sixteen feet to the very top of the tower. The lighthouse built at Cap des Rosier is only a few feet taller. As the French Canadian masons entered through the small entrance at the base of the tower each morning, they had the distinct impression that they were entering a great stone fortress. Laid right on bedrock, the limestone stone wall was over six feet thick at the base. They made a masterful job of the limestone as it was cut and fitted together tightly. The exposed stone face was finished with firebrick.

The bare masonry may have been a reasonable approach for lighthouses built on the Great Lakes or the St. Lawrence River, but it proved quite inadequate there on the south coast of Labrador, exposed to the extreme effects of wind and sea spray. In a report tabled in the House of Commons, the Superintendent wrote, "...it was deemed advisable...to cover (it) over with clapboards to prevent the action of the weather destroying it, as it was found that the severe frost and easterly winds to which (it was) subjected had a very injurious effect on the stonework." Three years after the completion of the lighthouse, a system of oak planks was attached to the masonry. These planks served as a nailing surface for cedar shingles that completely sheathed the tower.

A wooden stair wound one hundred and twenty-two steps up to the lantern room. The stair was broken by a series of eight landings, each having a narrow window offering a spectacular view of the coastline. The lantern room was built using cast iron; the roof was copper. The details of this space were beautifully crafted right down to Victorian gargoyles that stared serenely out to sea. The Quebec Trinity House had "a high class French dioptric light of the 2nd Order" installed in the lantern room. It is not clear who built this huge 55 inch wide light mechanism. It is believed that it came from the famous French firm of Barbier et Turenne who supplied a similar apparatus at the Cap des Rosier Lighthouse. Five large, flat wick lamps would consume about two hundred gallons of whale oil each shipping season. These lamps exhibited a fixed white light that could be seen as far as eighteen miles up and down the Strait.

A stone residence was constructed next to the lighthouse connected by a covered walkway. The one and one half storey structure had over 2,500 square feet of livable space, making it quite substantial by contemporary standards. Seventy years later, the building was divided into two living areas each with its own entrance. The steeply pitched roof was shingled with pine shakes.

Few records remain concerning the first ten years of operation at the lighthouse at Point Amour. Monsieur Blampied from Quebec was the first keeper there. Beyond the typical keeper's activities, Blampied had to contend with the problems of firing a signal gun during the frequent periods of foggy weather at Point Amour. Blampied and his assistant fired the "nine pounder" once every hour in foggy weather. Amazingly, they used nearly a ton of powder annually. When Blampied died in the spring of 1869, Captain Pierre Godier took over as head keeper.

The system of using the signal gun proved to be an ineffective method for warning mariners lost in the fogs off Point Amour. In 1877, the Canadian Department of Marine and Fisheries decided to relocate an existing fog alarm operating at Cape Ray on the southwest coast of Newfoundland to Point Amour. The following year, the ten inch steam whistle was erected near the village of L'Anse Amour, a mile or so west of the lighthouse. A small brook supplied the steam boiler with necessary water. The boiler used one hundred and thirty tons of coal a year. This coal had to be shipped from Montreal each year, landed and carted to the fog alarm station. The signal gun was relocated to the lighthouse station on Greenly Island near Blanc Sablon.

Pierre Godier died in the spring of 1880. It was not until September of that year that M. Thomas Wyatt became the new keeper at Point Amour. Thomas and later his son Jeff Wyatt would be responsible for the lighthouse over the next eighty years. In 1888, the Wyatt's were

"Point Amour Lighthouse, 1887."

honoured with a visit from Rev. Michael F. Howley, the Vicar of St. George's. Later, Rev. Howley would become the Archbishop of St. John's. Rev. Howley observed that Thomas Wyatt was interested in natural history and managed to collect an assortment of artifacts from the wild during his many walks along this magnificent shore. Wyatt was also known as a bit of a tinker occupying his free time working on various inventions in his workshop.

Thomas Wyatt for all of his eccentricities proved that he could be called upon to think fast and get a difficult job done. In the fall of 1889, he would be credited with saving the lives of four men from the wreck of HMS *Lily*. The *Lily* was a 720 ton gun boat that was powered both by sail and by steam engine. Built in Scotland in 1874 for the Royal Navy, she was part of the North American Squadron stationed in Bermuda. The *Lily* was off the south coast of Labrador attempting to intercept the mail ship enroute from Montreal for Great Britain. On September 16, she lay in a heavy sea off the coast lost in a thick sea fog. The problem was further complicated by dense smoke caused by a huge forest fire that burned out of control inland. In the late afternoon, Captain Gerald Russell could hear the steam whistle at Point Amour sounding at what appeared to be some distance from the ship. He chose not to alter course and a few minutes later the *Lily* ran straight into a reef just below the lighthouse.

The ship struck with such force that sailors were thrown from the rigging. The hull was stove in, and she immediately began filling with water. One lifeboat capsized in the heavy surf breaking offshore. While seven men drowned in the freezing water, most in this lifeboat did managed to swim ashore. The twenty-five men aboard a second lifeboat chose to wait offshore overnight rather than risk the perilous trip through the breakers. The next morning, the hull of the *Lily* had sunk to the bottom, only her masts remained above the sea. Four men still clung there in the rigging in hopes of a rescue from shore. It was Thomas Wyatt who rigged a bosun's chair and managed to get a line to the ship. Thomas Wyatt's heroism and ingenuity was mentioned in the Annual Report of the Canadian Department of Marine and Fisheries. The Lord Commissioners of the British Admiralty gave Wyatt a fine mantle clock as a gift in recognition of his actions.

Two years later, the first compressed air diaphone was erected at Point Amour replacing the steam whistle built further to the west. The foundation of this building still remains on a site just one hundred and sixty feet below the lighthouse at the very edge of the shore. The boilers of the fog alarm were replaced in 1906 and again in 1914. It was during these years that other changes took place at Point Amour. In 1903, the beacon was changed from a fixed white light to an occulting one.... 16 seconds light, 4 seconds eclipse. The old whale oil lamps were replaced with new kerosene burners. Wyatt complained to the Ministry that he had trouble keeping the new ones properly adjusted. The Department had considered the construction of a steam generated electric light plant for the lighthouse but found that there wasn't enough water available to supply the boiler. Telegraph lines were run from the North Shore of Quebec to Point Amour and on to Red Bay in 1901. Three years later, the Canadian Government built a "wireless" radio station at Point Amour. With a two hundred mile range, a station at Point Amour meant that sea traffic inbound from ports in Europe could wire ahead to the "Marconi" station at Point Amour. Messages could then be relayed by telegraph ahead to Montreal and Toronto.

Thomas Wyatt and his wife Emma had three children; two boys and a girl. His oldest son, Jeff, took over as keeper in 1919 when he was 24.

Only three years later, the young keeper was to witness one of the most spectacular shipwrecks ever to take place near one of the Newfoundland lighthouses. The HMS *Raleigh*, a newly commissioned Light Cruiser, was the proud flagship of the North American Squadron. She was considered "state of the art" in 1922. Over six hundred feet long, the graceful ship with her long, tapered bow could cut through the water at thirty knots. She had an armament of seven 7.5-inch guns and a complement of seven hundred officers and crew.

In the summer of 1922, the *Raleigh* departed with other Squadron ships on a courtesy tour of American and Canadian ports. The Commander of the Fleet, Admiral Pakenham on board the HMS *Calcutta*, decided to extend the tour to visit Newfoundland. In the first week of August, they arrived at Corner Brook stopping in the harbour at Curling. From there, they travelled up the Northern Peninsula stopping in St. Anthony before heading on down to St. John's.

It seems that British Naval officers on board the *Raleigh* had a penchant for a "spot" of fishing on the Labrador. As they passed through the Strait, Captain Bromley decided to alter course and make for Forteau Bay. The Forteau River was known for its trout and salmon fishing. Unfortunately, the unpredictable currents and the thick fogs of the Strait proved to be more than a match for those on board the *Raleigh*.

It had been a particularly bad year for icebergs. Even in August several bergs still drifted down through the Strait of Belle Isle from the Davis Strait. The *Raleigh* encountered one in the fog as they neared the entrance of Forteau Bay. They altered the ship's course nearer to shore to avoid the massive obstacle. Everyone on board held their breath as they passed the Point Amour Fog Alarm. It sounded loudly just off their starboard side. Luck was not with them that August afternoon. The sleek hull of the warship was ripped down her length by the jagged limestone reef that lay just two hundred metres west of the lighthouse. The mass of the 12,000 ton ship carried her in over the same reef that had claimed the HMS *Lily* thirty-three years before. The warship began to settle quickly into the shallow water of the reef.

"HMS Raleigh on shore."

Captain Bromley ordered a motorboat over the side in an attempt to get a line ashore. While there was no real sea on that evening, the lifeboat was capsized in the surf and ten sailors drowned in the accident. One man did manage to make it ashore with the line. It was quickly made secure with the help of Jeff Wyatt and the other men at the station.

The small groups of the crew climbed into light canvas lifeboats, and pulling themselves hand over hand, managed to transfer safely to shore. It must have been quite an evening at the station as the keeper and his

"Point Amour Lighthouse and fog alarm."

family attempted to bunk down seven hundred men. Jeff Wyatt found a place for them all in the little village of sheds, workshops and lighthouse buildings that were scattered over the grassy ridge. Five days later, the SS *Montrose*, a CPR liner arrived from Montreal to take the crew back to England. By then, they were scattered up and down the Strait, billeted in a number of communities along the shore.

The Admiralty intended to resist the plunder of their ship by residents of the Strait and did manage to get most of the militarily-sensitive items off the *Raleigh*. They eventually abandoned the warship to the wreckers. A multitude of small boats appeared from both sides of the Strait, and they began to strip her of anything that had value.

Those on board the *Raleigh* on the first day after she had been abandoned made a quite discovery. It was a find that is remembered to this very day. There was an ancient British tradition to administer a daily toddy of rum to every member of the crew. The wreckers discovered hundreds of gallons of the finest West Indian rum in her holds still intact. This wonderful cache together with huge stores of food meant that many coastal communities enjoyed a very merry Christmas that year. One community on the tip of the Northern Peninsula even changed their name in honour of the mighty warship.

The whole affair was quite an embarrassment to the British Admiralty. The wreck lay grounded on the reef in clear view of all those ships which passed in and out of the Strait of Belle Isle. Four years later, they sent a demolition team out to Point Amour to complete the job that had been begun by the sea. When they departed, the *Raleigh* was left dismembered, strewn all along the shore below the lighthouse.

Typhoid fever broke out at Point Amour in the spring of 1925; Jeff Wyatt fell ill to this deadly disease first. The wireless operator, his wife and two children quickly became infected. It was only through the tireless efforts of the medical staff from the nursing station at Forteau that the keeper and the others managed to survive the illness.

The Point Amour Lighthouse station was involved in another international event in the spring of 1928. In April of that year, a German expedition was the first to fly non-stop across the Atlantic Ocean from east to west. The crew of two Germans and an Irishman first made North America somewhere along the southeast coast of Labrador. Low on fuel after their thirty-seven

"Jeff Wyatt during the war years."

hour trip, they crash landed the *Bremen*, their Junkers monoplane, on Greenly Island west of Point Amour near the community of Blanc Sablon. The wireless operator at Point Amour signalled the news to the world. The German plane was recovered and placéd in the Ford Museum in Dearbourn, Michigan, where it remains today.

Jeff Wyatt retired in 1961 after keeping the lighthouse at Point Amour for forty-five years. Milton Elliot operated the lighthouse through most of the 1960s. In 1964, the old kerosene lanterns that had been installed at the turn of the century were finally replaced by a 400 Watt Mercury Va-

"Aerial photo of Point Amour Light-house station."

courtesy Public Archives, Newfoundland & Labrador

pour lamp. During those days the Point Amour station was more like a small town with twenty-five to thirty people living there. Three assistant keepers worked with Elliot to maintain this large facility. The radio operator and his family were the fifth household living at the station.

Max Sheppard became the head keeper in 1969 after working as the first assistant for five years under Mr. Elliot. With automation of the lighthouse and the closing of the radio office in the 1970s, the population at the station began to decline.

The 1970s saw a huge influx of workers associated with the construction of a tunnel beneath the Strait of Belle Isle. This tunnel was not intended for vehicular travel but rather to allow the transmission of electrical power from the Churchill Falls Hydroelectric Station to the Island. The narrowest point of the Strait actually exists between Point Amour and Flower's Cove on the Great Northern Peninsula. With only sixteen kilometres across the Strait, the bureaucrats reasoned that it was the most economical place to cut the tunnel. Hundreds of men were assembled at each end of the tunnel. A shaft was begun, and a series of large storage buildings were constructed. The project was abandoned after only a few years without completing the tunnel. They spent sixty-seven million dollars on the scheme before they called a halt to the construction.

In the early 1980s, the project's facilities were sold at auction and removed from the site. One building still remains there, a monument to the ingenuity and resourcefulness of the people of the Straits. A Regional Recreation Association was formed by the towns in the area. This

Association purchased the largest warehouse on the site and converted it into a natural ice arena. While not ideally located for such a purpose, it has served the region well for hockey in the winter months and various summer activities including their annual Bakeapple Festival.

In 1980, the last assistant keeper departed from the Point Amour Lighthouse station. The lighthouse became a one man operation when it was made completely automatic. When Max Sheppard retires, the station will probably become an unmanned station.

In some ways the Point Amour Lighthouse is the most isolated of those considered in this book. The journey is also the most satisfying for those who would take the time to travel to this magical place. At Deer Lake follow the Viking Trail (Route 430) north through the Gros Morne National Park and beyond past a series of outport communities. The drive along the western edge of the Great Northern Peninsula is most beautiful. It takes about three and a half hours to travel from Deer Lake to the ferry terminal at St. Barbe. The ferry departs from here for the crossing of the Strait. In the summer there are only two crossings a day, each taking nearly two hours. There are lineups so you should plan ahead to make sure you are there in time.

The ferry lands in Blanc Sablon, a fishing village on the Quebec side of the border. From the Terminal access road, turn east toward the Labrador border and the first in a chain of communities that make up the area known as *the Straits*. Travel along Route 510, passing first through L'Anse au Clair, then on toward Forteau. About seventeen kilometres from the ferry terminal, on top of a high headland, you will glimpse the magnificent site of Point Amour Lighthouse across Forteau Bay. Continue east through Forteau and English Point.

If you continue another seventy kilometres down Route 510, you will eventually come to the community of Red Bay. It was here in 1977 that archaeologists discovered the extensive remains of a historic Basque whaling station. The station operated from this excellent harbour each summer between 1550 and 1600. A long, low island known as Saddle Island spans the entrance of that harbour. It acts as a natural wind and sea break from the torment of the North Atlantic. It was on this island that the archaeologists discovered several sites for the tryworks used to reduce the whale blubber to oil. Also, a cemetery was discovered at one end of Saddle Island, facing the open sea. It contained the remains of Basque fishermen who had died in their efforts to harpoon the great whales. The Basque journals of the day mentioned the wreck of one of the large supply vessels that was to carry the wooden barrels of whale oil back to their homeland. Divers found the well preserved wreck of the *San Juan* in thirty feet of water on the leeward side of Saddle Island.

Both the Provincial and Federal governments undertook extensive excavations of the many sites in Red Bay during the 1980s. In 1989, an interpretive centre was built on the shore of the harbour. It is from here you can take a five minute boat ride to visit the historic island.

At about twenty-eight kilometres from the ferry terminal, you will notice a gravel road off to your right. Turn here, and travel down to the lighthouse. There is an important archaeological site about one and a half kilometres from the highway intersection. On your right heading south toward the lighthouse, you should watch for a modest plaque that marks the location of a grave of a little Indian child who died 7500 years ago. The burial site was hidden in the sand dune thickets behind the large sweeping beach known as L'Anse Amour. It is no more than a low sandy mound covered with beach stones. Two archaeologists from Memorial University discovered the site in 1973, as they were scouring the south coast of Labrador for evidence of the Maritime Archaic Indians. James Tuck and Robert McGhee reasoned that this beach area would serve as an excellent camp site for these prehistoric Indians in their pursuit of harp seals on the winter iceflows offshore.

Tuck and McGhee carefully excavated the grave, digging down through successive layers of sand and stone. About five feet below the surface, they found the remains of the child's skeleton. He lay face down with a flat rock across his back. His body was anointed with red ochre. His family had placed an assortment of objects around the child. These articles included a bone necklace and a whistle made from the bone of a sea bird. Several stone knives were placed around his body as well.

Tuck and McGhee discovered the remnants of two fires lit beside him. The charcoal from these fires was carbon dated to between 7000 and 7500 years ago. This grave is perhaps the oldest aboriginal burial site found in North America. McGhee wrote in their report, "As far as we know at present, no peoples on earth were taking such pains in disposing of their dead in this manner at that time - a period that preceded the building of the Egyptian pyramids by more than 2000 years." The grave was returned to its original state after the archaeologists completed their study.

You should proceed another kilometre and a half through the village of L'Anse Amour to the Point Amour Lighthouse. At the edge of the village, you should stop and visit a small cemetery located there. You will note a large granite tombstone that commemorated the death of the ten sailors from the *Raleigh*. Travel the last kilometre along the narrow road that runs at the bottom of an ancient cliff. You are so close to the water that storm waves break over it in the winter.

The lighthouse is magnificent, built on a grassy meadow overlooking the Strait of Belle Isle. The one hundred and twenty foot stone tower is in excellent condition. The original keeper's duplex stands next to the tower. Several bungalows remain within the complex. The fog alarm and a storage shed housing a diesel generator also can be found there. The

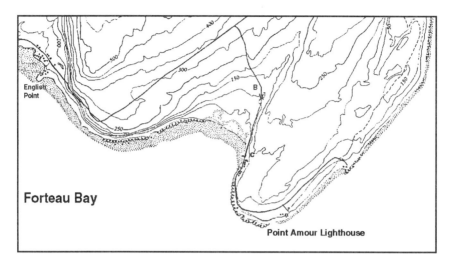

Forteau Bay

English Point

B

C

Point Amour Lighthouse

amiable Max Sheppard is the present keeper. He joined the Canadian Coast Guard in 1959 and was appointed keeper in 1969. He is quite happy to show a visitor around the historic lighthouse complex.

Take time to walk down to the wreck of the *Raleigh*. Follow a grassy path that runs parallel to the shore, between the abandoned residences to a wire gate at the far side of the compound. The overgrown lane is all that remains of the original roadway that connected the community of Forteau with the Point Amour lighthouse. Walk from the gate, west, back in time to the site of the wreck of the *Raleigh*. The skeleton of the great warship lies there today on a jagged limestone reef just a few minutes walk from the lighthouse.

Cape Race
(Flash .25 seconds; eclipse 7.25 seconds)
The Landfall Light

"Our ship is now waiting, her anchor she's weighing
Farewell to the land that I'm going to leave;
My Betsy has parted with father and mother,
With me for to cross o'er the wide western wave.
So hasten dear Betsy, my dear blue-eyed lassie,
Bid farewell to Mother and come with me;
I'll do my endeavour to make your heart cheery,
Till we reach the green fields of Americay."

Anonymous

C aptain Edward Rose stood on the stone wharf in Rotterdam harbour and watched as the sixteen German families slowly climbed the gangway to board his old ship. It was a motley group to be sure, clutching their few threadbare possessions close to their breasts. He wondered if his *Florence* would be up to the task one more time. The aging brigantine had been built thirty years before, to take advantage of the new trade between Europe and the New England States after the end of the War of 1812. For years, he had guided his ship to ports in England and France loaded with timber from his native New England or cotton from the Southern States. On her return trips, the holds would be filled with the finished goods of Europe for the New York market. In recent years though, he found a more profitable trade in transporting these pitiable immigrants to New York.

The *Florence* had definitely not been built to carry passengers. The Germans would have to use the ship's cargo hold, the conditions there were cramped to say the least. Each family would receive a berth no bigger than ten square feet. They would receive only dry biscuit and stale water for sustenance. The good Captain would receive £5 for every man, woman and child who crossed in *steerage*. Captain Rose did not see any reason to increase the number of lifeboats stowed on board.

If the weather stayed good, he could let them spend as much time on deck as possible. It was the winter crossings which Ross hated, for they had to be confined below deck in the dark foul holds. The hatches had to be tied down to prevent the winter sea from flooding them.

Raised in the new democracy of America, it never ceased to amaze him why these poor people left their homes in droves and endured those miserable four weeks in the holds of his ship. On these crossings, as many as a quarter of the emigrants would die, mostly the old and the young, succumbing to ship fever (cholera) or malnutrition or the horrors of the winter crossing. The industrious American shrugged these thoughts off; he could surely make more money shipping emigrants than Indian tea on his westward trip. The reality was that most of these Europeans were fleeing the political chaos that swept through Europe after the final defeat of Napoleon. This human tide was just beginning in the first quarter of the nineteenth century, it would grow to a flood as famine and religious persecution drove millions to America in search of a new life.

With the last family on board, Captain Rose went below to his cabin to consider the crossing he had made so many times before. After hopefully a quick passage through the crowded English Channel, he would turn his ship west for the long two thousand mile leg of the journey to the New World. With God's grace, he would attempt to make his first landfall at a dreadful headland know as Cape Race on the southeast coast of Newfoundland. Having safely made this lonely place, he would re-adjust his course southwest for the final one thousand mile leg making New York ten days later.

By 1840, Cape Race had become one of the great landmarks of North America for it was the first landfall seen by the millions of emigrants crossing the Atlantic. Little did Captain Rose know that the early Breton and Basque fisherman had been using Cape Race as their landfall for more than three hundred years. It was first noted on a map printed in 1502 as Cape Raso. Jacques Cartier called it Cap de Raze in 1536. The most westerly point on the coast of Brittany is also called Cap Raz. The term *radere* or *rasum* means to shave. It seems that these early fishermen liked to apply this name to any prominent Cape which ended a certain coastline, and which had to be rounded in order to get free wind. As master mariners, they would sail their vessels so close to the point that they are said to have shaved it.

Captain Rose had no intention of shaving by Cape Race, as soon as he identified this terrible place, he would quickly alter his course to avoid it. He had to trust to his navigating skills and the telltale signs of land birds to warn him of their approach. Some times in the summer, he could tell that he was getting close by the warm fragrant southwest winds that carried the tang of fir and spruce forests.

As the 200 ton square rigger slipped her lines and eased out of the Dutch harbour, Captain Rose couldn't help to feel some misgivings. He knew that those same southwest winds could mean sea fogs off Cape Race. These dense fogs were formed as the warm, moist land winds met the icy ocean current that flowed down the coast of Labrador from the Baffin Sea. The whole coastline had the reputation as "the Graveyard of the Atlantic" as many ships met their fate at that dreadful headland. Captain Rose knew that there were treacherous currents which could drag unsuspecting ships into a wide rocky bay know as Trepassey that lay just to the south of Cape Race. Trepassey Bay had also been named by the Basque fishermen, roughly translated, it meant the "bay of death" or "bay of lost souls."

He knew that the Cape Spear lighthouse lay further to the north. It has operated for the past five years to mark the entrance to St. John's Bay. Captain Rose couldn't understand why the British Admiralty wouldn't establish a lighthouse where most ships travelling between North America and Europe made their first landfall.

Early on the morning of August 9, 1840, Captain Rose stood uneasily at the helm of the *Florence*. The ship had been at sea for four weeks. His dead reckoning told him that Cape Race had to be near, but as he had feared, the entire coastline was enveloped in a dense sea fog. The ship was lost, why he could barely see the sailor he had ordered to the bowsprit to act as lookout. He never saw the black cliffs of Cape Race until it was too late, the *Florence* struck just one mile west of Cape Race going full out. While the winds were light that morning, they were enough to smash the brigantine against the jagged cliffs. As the towering masts toppled like great pine trees in a tangle of canvas and rigging, Captain Rose knew that his old ship would not hold together. He knew also that the two lifeboats on board would not be able to hold all eighty-seven people. He ordered the women and children into the two frail boats and away. Just in time, for the hull broken in many places, began to settle immediately. Forty-nine souls, including Captain Rose died quickly in the icy water.

The survivors in the lifeboats scrambled on to a sea swept ledge at the base of the vertical one hundred and fifty foot cliff. Slowly they made their way up until finally, exhausted from their ordeal, they reached the top. The miserable party found themselves at the edge of a great treeless plateau completely devoid of any sign of habitation. Their clothes in tatters, they wandered lost in this wilderness living only on the berries that they could find. Curious herds of caribou watched from the horizon as they slowly made their way northward along the high cliffs. Four days after the wreck of the *Florence*, they were found by humble fishermen from the tiny village of Renews. There they were feed and cared for until they were taken by boat to St. John's.

Stories of the hardship and suffering faced by these women and children swept quickly through the Town. The inhabitants took pity on the survivors and "subscribed a handsome sum to provide (for their) relief". Some of the orphaned children were adopted by local families; the rest were eventually given passage to New York.

This tragic shipwreck caused the Commissioners of Lighthouses in St. John's to redouble their efforts to have a lighthouse built on the southeast coast of the Avalon Peninsula. It appears though that their priority was with Cape Pine for they were more concerned with Newfoundland ships travelling around the south coast of the island.

The British Admiralty certainly realized the importance of Cape Race to trans-atlantic shipping for they had been loosing ships there for one hundred and fifty years. In 1847, Captain Bayfield was sent out to locate the site for the lighthouse at Cape Pine. He was also instructed survey Trepassey Bay and the headlands that lay to the north in the area of Cape Race. In the summer of 1851, a wooden "beacon" was erected at the very tip of Cape Race by a gang of English carpenters sent over from Cape Pine. This beacon was unlit and unmanned and proved to be quite ineffective.

In the fall of 1854, two spectacular accidents finally caused the British government to agree to build a lighthouse at Cape Race. Early in September of that year, another American emigrant ship *City of Philidelphia* went ashore in fog at Chance Cove just to the north of Cape Race. The ship was bound for Philadelphia from Liverpool with 540 people on board. Luckily for those on the ship, the seas were calm, and they all managed to make it safely to the long cobblestone beach. This huge party was forced to camp where they had landed until help arrived from Renews. Chandler White, a local merchant petitioned the Newfoundland House of Assembly after this accident,

"Sir,

I beg leave respectfully to call the attention of the government to the great benefit that would arise from the establishment of a Light House on Cape Race.

The recent wreck of a splendid Steamer, with near six hundred souls on board, from Liverpool, bound to Philadelphia, near that place, having been brought to the particular notice of the government, presents a sufficient excuse, I trust, for urging upon your consideration, a subject which deeply interest, not only those of this colony and of all commercial nations who have lives and property at risk on this coast, but the philanthropic and benevolent of every land.

Cape Race is the point on the great highway of nations, towards which every mariner bound on either the eastern or western voyage between Europe and America, looks as to a place of departure, it being nearly in the line of the great circle-sailing, between the ports of Liverpool, London, and Havre, on the one side of the Atlantic; and Boston, New York, and Philadelphia on the other.

In view of the millions of lives and property the safety of which would be greatly increased if the suggestion be carried into effect, it seems superfluous to enlarge upon the want of a Light House on this most prominent Cape; I beg leave respectfully to ask you, to submit to His Excellency the Governor, a proposition to remove the Beacon at present on Cape Race, to Mistaken Point and that a *first class Light* be established in lieu thereof.

I have the honour to be, with great respect

Sir,

Your most obedient servant

Chandler White, J.P."

Only a couple of weeks after the *City of Philidelphia* was wrecked, a terrible collision took place in fog off the crowded waters off Cape Race. The *Artic*, a 2,800 ton paddle steamer struck the *Vesta*, a French ship. The *Artic*, built only four years before, was part of the Collins Line, carried 381 passengers and crew and was bound for Britain from New York. Built of wood, she was badly holed by the iron ship, and began to sink. In the panic that ensued, less than a quarter of all those on board made it to life rafts. Over three hundred people died.

The next spring, the British Secretary of State wrote Governor LeMarchant in St. John's,

"Sir,

The importance of building a Light House at Cape Race, Newfoundland, having attracted the attention of Her Majesty's Government, I have to inform you that Parliament will be asked this session to apply a sum of £5000 for that purpose.

It is not at present determined whether the Light House shall be of Iron or of Stone; but should it be built of the former material, no time will be lost in its construction, and if possible, it will be conveyed to the colony in sufficient time to allow of its being in action before the ensuing winter.

Her Majesty's Government will be prepared to defray one half of the expense of maintaining the proposed Light, but it is considered that the remaining money may properly devolve upon the colony, which will derive essential advantage form its establishment.

I have the honour to be, with great respect

Sir,

Your most obedient servant

Sir George Grey

Downing Street, 3rd April, 1855"

Throughout the summer of 1855, there was a fair amount of correspondence between various British government offices and the Colonial Government in St. John's. Oke argued for an iron structure as it "appears to be the most durable, suitable and the most economical for Buildings of this nature". The Secretary of State finally agree to this plan but insisted that "the dwellings of the Light Keepers, if constructed of Stone or Brick about the base of the Tower, would be perfectly unobjectionable".

Alexander Gordon, the civil engineer from London was given the contract to design the iron tower for Cape Race. He had prepared the design of the Cape Pine lighthouse tower six years before. Gordon proposed a relatively narrow structure this time, having a height of forty feet. Oke later explained, "The tower....is surrounded by a stone wall - the space between the tower and wall, nine feet, (and) is laid off into six apartments as a residence for the keepers."

"The ice off Cape Race."

Drawn by C. Graham for *Harper's Weekly*, April 15, 1885

Thirty-two iron plates were cast in England and shipped to Trepassey that fall. They were then carted to the one hundred and twenty-five foot high rocky finger known as Cape Race. The new lighthouse was

106

to be build beside the beacon that had been erected in 1851. It took twenty men all the next summer to hoist the 3/4 ton panels into position. Eight hundred bolts held the structure tightly together. Red and white vertical stripes were painted on the tower.

The light mechanism was installed in the fall. It was initially a fixed light having eight catoptric reflectors, lit by Argand lamps. This initial light had a fairly low illuminance with a mere 6,000 foot candles. The total cost of the project was said to be £5,160.

From the start, the British Colonial Office acknowledged the importance of the Light at Cape Race. They eventually agreed to cover all of the costs of the operation of the light, some £430 per year. The British had been taxing all shipping, one shilling per ton annually, to defray operating costs of their lighthouses. Starting in 1855, an additional 1/16 shilling per ton was imposed annually on every ship making trans-atlantic crossings. These funds were then sent to the Colonial Government in St. John's for their use.

The Colonial Government appointed a retired Captain, William Hally to be the first keeper at Cape Race. The light was first exhibited on December 15, 1856. Amazingly, Hally was to play a significant role in a shipwreck to take place only ten days later. He must have been just finishing his Christmas supper with his family when distress flares lit the sky. They were signals from the *Welsford* which had departed from Saint John, New Brunswick ten days earlier heavy with timber bound for Liverpool.

Cape Race had been enveloped in a very dense fog all day. Even with the new lighthouse operating, the *Welsford* did not have a chance. Lost in the dark, she struck the reef right below the lighthouse at 6 pm. A heavy swell ground the ship against the one hundred and twenty foot black shale cliff. Captain Hally and his assistant cast lines down to the men and managed to save four of the crew. The remainder of the crew, all twenty-two died that Christmas night.

Haunted by this most recent accident, life at the station was to get even more miserable. The design of the stone residence, build around the perimeter of the iron lighthouse proved quite unworkable. Oke wrote, "the smoke was intolerable and every effort in the way of remedy proved abortive. Add to this the walls and tower were with every change of weather either steaming with damp or coated with ice."

The following year the British Government agreed to build a wooden residence with a covered way connecting it with the lighthouse. In 1858, Captain Hally and his new assistant George Hewitt gratefully moved into the new residence "replete with every comfort and convenience."

During these early years, Cape Race became quite famous for another reason beyond its reputation as the great wrecker of ships. By 1856, after several unsuccessful attempts, a telegraph line was completed between New York and St. John's. The following year the New York Associated Press hatched a plan which would allow them to get news from the Continent a week before any other paper. The plan would see the stationing of mailboats off Cape Race, they were to intercept newsbags dropped off by trans-atlantic steamers passing the headland. These bags were transferred to Cape Race, and then relayed through St. John's and on to New York by the newly completed telegraph line. On stormy days, when the mailboats could not make a transfer, the newsbags would be placed into barrels and unceremoniously dumped into the sea for the fishermen to pick up. The fisherman all knew that they would receive £5 sterling for every barrel that they could safely deliver to Cape Race, a fortune for them in those days.

This arrangement also worked in reverse as well. Frequently, residents in St. John's wishing to travel to Britain, would make their way to Cape Race. They hoped to make a perilous transfer on board one of those steamers headed back across the Atlantic. This flurry of activity in the waters off Cape Race after the lighthouse was built could only heighten the prominence of the station in the eyes of both the Colonial and British governments. Five years later, a shipwreck was to take place near by which would catapult Cape Race into headlines around the world.

Since the early nineteenth century, the emigrant trade had been growing in leaps and bounds. By the middle of the century, millions of emigrants began leaving Continental Europe for America. Millions left Ireland alone in the late 1840s and 50s, starved out of their homeland by the famine created by the failure of their potato crops. British, American and Canadian businessmen attempting to capitalize on the phenomenon began building swift steamships capable of handling hundreds of emigrant families in steerage. The *Anglo-Saxon* was one of these ships. She was built in Dumbarton, Scotland in 1860 for the Allen Line. Sheathed in iron, and driven by great steam engines, she was also fully rigged for sail, carrying three full masts.

The *Anglo-Saxon* departed out of Liverpool in early April, 1863, on board were four hundred and forty-six people, three hundred and sixty of these were emigrants. The crossing proceeded normally, but as they approached the coast of Newfoundland, the heavy weather set in. It was foggy of course, with a heavy sea that had been built by a storm the day before. The wind had moderated to the southwest. It was miserably cold with rain showers. The situation was complicated by the fact that the *Anglo-Saxon* had begun encountering fairly heavy pan ice, so common in the spring of the year off Cape Race.

On the morning of April 27, 1863, Captain Burgess stood in his bridge and peered into the fog. He knew that Cape Race had to be near and ordered the engine room to reduce speed. He listened to the ebbing throb of his engines and the rattle of the cold rain on the forward windows. It was said later that Burgess had hoped to call in at Cape Race in order to find out the ice conditions in the Gulf of St. Lawrence. The ship was bound for Quebec City.

Suddenly at 11:10 am, right in front of the great steamer a shallow cove appeared through the fog. Known as Clam Cove by local fishermen, it was fringed by low cliffs, atop were dense thickets of stunted spruce. Burgess ordered the engines reversed, but the ship did not respond fast enough, and gliding between two great rocks offshore, she grounded on a black reef. The Captain tried to back the *Anglo-Saxon* off the ledge. But as she did, the stern turned inward and the ship became pinned on first, one rock at the stern and then the other at the bow. As the huge sea began to break over the ship, Captain Burgess knew his ship was done for and ordered his crew to ready the lifeboats.

The fact was there were only enough lifeboats for half of those on board. One boat did manage to get away, but a second one fully loaded with passengers was smashed with rigging which had fallen from one of the masts. Quickly, three more boats got away as the ship began to break up pounded by gigantic swells. Tied to a line, three of the crew leaped over the landward side of the steamer and swam the one hundred metres to shore. A heavier line was then drawn ashore and a bosun's chair rigged. Captain Hally and his new assistant George Hewitt, alerted by the wail of the stricken ship's whistle, made their way to the site some four miles north of the lighthouse. They used hand lines to climb down and helped rescue the eighty or so miserable survivors stranded at the base of the cliff.

As they watched, the great iron liner capsized. Slipping off the two rocks that had held her for such a short time, the *Anglo-Saxon* sank in deeper water. Many of those who died, were clinging to the rigging of the ship waiting rescue. They were dragged down into the icy water, tangled in the mess of sheets and tackle and booms. Two hundred and thirty-seven people, mostly emigrants, died on that dark water. Captain Burgess went down with his ship. More than one hundred of the bodies recovered could not be identified. Captain Hally buried them on the cliff over-looking the site of the wreck. Their graves are marked with twin beach stones at the head and the foot.

In the inquiry that took place after the tragedy, the Allen Line was criticized for not having sufficient lifeboats on board. They realized that the dense fog often made the lighthouse ineffective. The need for a fog alarm at Cape Race was identified as being essential to reduce the number of accidents there.

Robert Oke commented, "From Chance Cove to the east point of Trepassey Bay, the distance of sixteen miles, and in that space there have been yearly more disastrous shipwrecks and loss of life than the whole of the remaining portions of our coast put together." He recommended switching the characteristics of the lights at Cape Race and Cape Pine across Trepassey Bay.

"In consequence of representation made to their Lordships, the Committee of Privy Council for Trade, to the light at Cape Race as being of too feeble a power and circumscribed range for so an important a Head Land, their Lordships have had under consideration, the expediency of altering Cape Race's fixed light to a revolving light, and Cape Pine's revolving light to a fixed light, providing each station with the means of exhibiting a more powerful and brilliant light that heretofore. I have as directed, had the honour to submit to their Lordships, an estimate of the expense consequent on the alteration, which I believe will be carried out in the course of the ensuing summer (1866)". Captain Hally retired that same summer, replaced by his son Michael. The assistant keeper, George Hewitt was transferred to Cape Pine taking over from Henry Hearder.

With Confederation in 1867, the British Admiralty's tenuous jurisdiction over Cape Race was transferred to the newly formed Canadian Department of Marine and Fisheries. While the Newfoundland government owned and operated the lighthouse at Cape Race, the Canadian government continued to subsidize the costs associated with the operation. In their first Annual Report, the Minister indicated the desire of the Government to construct a Fog Alarm at Cape Race.

In 1872, after considerable bickering between both governments, a "powerful" ten inch steam whistle was built on a site about two hundred and fifty metres from the lighthouse at the very edge of the cliff. The present day fog alarm still occupies the same site. This steam whistle was similar to the one built a few years before in Saint John, New Brunswick. A boiler engineer, Patrick Myrick was appointed to operate the steam whistle. He was the son of an Irishman who had emigrated from Tipperary to St. John's in the 1820s.

The arrangement with the Canadian Government did not last. The Department of Marine and Fisheries argued, "This lighthouse is indispensable to the safety of Canadian and other vessels navigating the North Atlantic to and from Canada, and by its transfer to Canada, the Dominion (would be) relieved from the payment of lighthouse dues which amount yearly to about $1,200." On July 1, 1886, the lighthouse station officially came under the control of the Department of Marine and Fisheries. There was over $100,000 in a fund set aside for the operation of the lighthouse. This was returned to the Canadian Government.

At the same time, Patrick Myrick, the fog alarm keeper became head keeper at Cape Race. Eleven years later, John Myrick took over from his father. Both men would see their share of wrecks in the vicinity of

Cape Race. It was reported that in the forty years between 1864 and 1904, over two thousand people lost their lives in 94 shipwrecks off Cape Race. The summer of 1901 was a particularly bad one, the hulls of ships were literally piling upon one another. On June 5, the *Assyrian*, a large steamer loaded with valuable freight from Antwerp went ashore in dense fog, a mile from the lighthouse. The Captain had mistaken the fog whistle for another ship. A small steamer named the *Petrel* fowled her tow line while attempting to pull the *Assyrian* off. Both ships sank after a week of battering by the relentless sea. Within weeks, the *Lusitania*, a French emigrant liner, struck a reef near Clam Cove in dense fog. The passengers reported later that many were thrown out of bed they struck so hard. All three hundred and sixty-four passengers and crew were safely transferred ashore with the help of John Myrick and his assistant. The schooner *Scottish Princess* and the steamer *Acis* were wrecked at Cape Race in August. Needless to say, the Canadian government was not particularly pleased with how things were going, it had never been satisfied with the physical characteristics of the Cape Race lighthouse. A number of changes took place at Cape Race over the next several years which would make it a world class lighthouse.

In 1904, the Canadian Government established a marine radio station at Cape Race on the hill overlooking the station. This "Marconi" station had a range of 300 to 400 miles, and could communicate with passing ships offshore using Morse Code. On April 14, 1912, the liner *Titanic* struck an iceberg 380 miles southeast of Cape Race. It was the Cape Race Radio Station which reported one of the world's worse marine accidents. One thousand and ninety people drowned because there were not sufficient lifeboats on board.

"Cape Race Lighthouse Station, 1910."

It was clear that several of the shipwrecks, which had taken place at Cape Race, were caused by the ship's crew mistaking the fog whistle for a ship's whistle. In 1907, the Canadian Government replaced the old whistle alarm with a new five inch diaphone alarm. The steam compressor which operated the fog alarm was said to be the largest in the world. The distinctive sound made by this system would surely be a help for those nearing the coast in dense fog.

In the same year, a new reinforced concrete lighthouse was built right next to the aging iron structure. At ninety-six feet, the beautifully proportioned lighthouse stood more than twice as high as the original tower. This concrete tower was the first to be commissioned by the Canadian Government. Its economical construction, durability and fire resistance meant that it would become the most commonly used system in the twentieth century.

An immense iron lantern standing twenty-five feet high, was set atop the tower. Beneath a dome sheathed in copper was housed one of the largest hyper-radical lens assemblies ever built. The light apparatus was built by Chance Brothers of Birmingham; the four complex lenses, each eight feet in diameter, were set securely in a gunmetal frame. A second smaller frame held an array of kerosene vapour lamps. This whole assembly weighed seven tons. In order to allow free movement, the mechanism "rested" on a cast iron pedestal: it "floated" in a trough containing almost half a ton of liquid mercury. This light mechanism is said to have a beam of light with an illumination equal to 1,500,000 foot candles, making it the most powerful lighthouse of its day.

Ironically, the original iron lighthouse was not destroyed. It was dismantled and shipped to Money Point at Cape North on the northeast tip of Cape Breton. For more than seventy years it provided its warning light to ships travelling into and out of the Gulf of St. Lawrence. In 1980, the Canadian Coast Guard decided to retire the iron structure, intending to replace it with an aluminum skeleton tower. The old lighthouse was dismantled one more time and air lifted to Ottawa. It had been donated to the National Museum of Science and Technology. In 1981, it was erected at the corner of St. Laurent Boulevard and Lancaster Road in suburban East Ottawa. It now stands across the corner from the Elmvale Mall, marking the entrance to the Museum's complex. Burger restaurants and doughnut shops mark its horizons now. Its flashing beams alternate with the stop lights at the intersection. The rumbling of the heavy traffic down the four lane highway has replaced the boom of long ocean swells against sheer rock cliffs.

The lighthouse station at Cape Race reached its zenith after the completion of the new tower, it had become a world class site. The station had grown to become a small community with as many as ten families living there at one time. William Myrick became the head keeper in the

1920s, making him the third Myrick to have that responsibility. The lighthouse and fog alarm were electrified in 1926, the power was supplied by two 50 HP boilers, fuelled by 500 tons of coal per year. A two-room school house was built for the dozens of children living there. There was even a small post office.

For the next forty years or so, through the two World Wars, the lighthouse station at Cape Race changed very little. The improved technology finally began to reduce the number of shipwrecks off the Cape. Eventually, improved marine navigation meant that ships did not need to use Cape Race as their first landfall. While it remained the crossroads of the trans-atlantic shipping lanes, mariners were finally able to avoid piling up on the black headland.

In 1944, Jim Myrick became the fourth and last descendant to be head keeper at Cape Race. He would be keeper for nearly thirty years, passing away in 1973. Tom Ryan became and still is the head keeper at Cape Race, Noel Myrick one of Jim's sons is one of the assistant keepers.

To visit Cape Race, you again must take the Southern Shore Road (Route 10) south from St. John's. The first leg of the trip will take about an hour and forty-five minutes. As you near the end of this drive, you cannot miss the twelve hundred foot high Loran C tower erected just off the highway. This tower serves as a navigational aid to both aircraft and shipping crossing the Atlantic. They use time difference measurements of signals emitted by this tower and other similar towers in Labrador, New Brunswick and New York to locate very precisely where they are.

Just past the Loran C tower, you will reach Portugal Cove South, about one hundred and forty kilometres from St. John's. Instead of travelling on to Trepassey, turn left there, driving through the fishing community, past the Government Wharf to the gravel road for Cape Race. It is about twenty-two kilometres from the village to the light-house, the drive will take about thirty minutes over a passable road. You will have to dodge quite a few potholes, and negotiate a couple of steep hills, but the drive is breathtaking. On your right, is Trepassey Bay, originally surveyed by Captain Henry Bayfield. On a clear day, you can just make out Cape Pine across the bay on the furthest point.

The first really steep hill (you'll know it when you get to it) takes you down to what used to be the community known as The Drook. In the old days, as many as nine families lived here. Mostly St. Croix's, they eked out an existence fishing. You can still see the stone foundations and remains of gardens. A beautiful black sand beach makes a perfect spot to enjoy a warm summer day in Newfoundland. This site wasn't so pleasant on May 5, 1936 when the banking schooner *Partanna* came ashore here in a violent storm. Twenty five crewmen were drowned.

A single string of power lines points the way across this barren landscape. Occasionally you will catch a glimpse of a wild seascape. The black shale and sandstone is often split to expose smooth planes thrust at angles out of the sea. Off to the right is a peninsula that ends in a headland known as Mistaken Point. It is named after the loss of countless ships that were drawn off course by the powerful currents into Trepassey Bay. Mistaken Point has become famous for another reason now. It seems that these shales were laid down over 620 million years ago. Fine river silts and sands swept down shallow river deltas, slowly deposited on the bottom of the warm Pre-Cambrian seas. These alluvial beds also received the fallout of ash from periodic volcanic eruptions. Many delicate frond-like marine organisms, jellyfish and the like, were trapped in the sediment and eventually fossilized. Mistaken Point is known for the outstanding Pre-Cambrian fossil remains, they are some of the oldest in the world. The Provincial Department of Environment and Lands has established an Ecological Reserve there. This designation will protect these fossils for future generations to enjoy. Just before you get to what remains of the community of Long Beach, you will pass a walking trail leading to Mistaken Point. A thirty minute walk will reward you with the sight of many beautiful fossils in the black shale.

The abandoned community of Long Beach is about six kilometres from Cape Race, many years ago four families of O'Neils lived there. All that remains today are stone foundations and several summer cottages owned by the descendants of these original families.

As you come around the last bend, in the distance you will see the proud, graceful presence of the Cape Race Lighthouse. It stands on a narrow peninsula which is thrust out from the rest of the coast, the enormous lens revolving inside the lantern can be easily seen from a great distance. Follow the road around the rocky cove that separates the peninsula from the coast. Drive past the lighthouse to the little parking area next to the keeper's residence and the fog alarm.

The large long bungalow right at the point, has always been the site for the keepers dwelling, there was a large two storey duplex residence there at the turn of the century. On the other side of the parking lot is the old fog alarm building. It ceased operation in 1991.

Just to the north side of the lighthouse is a very dangerous cut in the cliff. The ocean eroded the softer shale here. It has made a cut which drops two hundred feet straight into the sea. The spot is very dangerous, because you can't see it until you are right at the edge. So watch your children or your dogs that they might stray away and be lost.

Walk up to the knoll where the lighthouse is built. Tom Ryan or one of his staff is sure to take you inside. Eighty-five concrete stairs wind gracefully up the inside wall. An incredible echo makes it difficult to have a conversation as you climb. At the top, the huge lens assembly still rotates frictionlessly on the trough of mercury driven now by a 1/4

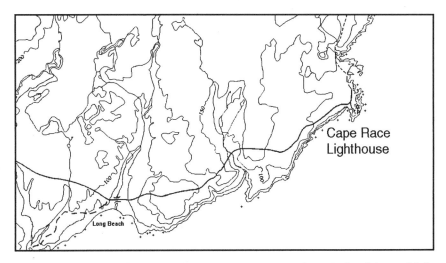

HP electric motor. It is a bit disconcerting, as the whole thing whirls silently around. The light is produced now by a single 400W Mercury Vapour light. This beacon exhibits a beam which can be seen thirty-two miles away, ended by the curvature of the earth.

From atop the tower now more than eighty years old, you can see the ragged coastline fall away off to the north. There, in one of those indentations four miles distant, lies Clam Cove. It is there that the liner *Anglo-Saxon* met her fate. You can still walk to the site of the wreck, skirting along the cliffs as Captain Hally must have done one hundred and thirty years ago.

Cape St. Mary's
(Flash 0.5 seconds; eclipse 4.5 seconds)
Bird Rock Light

Take me back to my Western boat.
Let me fish off Cape St. Mary's,
Where the hagdowns sail and the fog horns wail,
With my friends the Browns and the Clearys.
Let me fish off Cape St. Mary's.

Otto Kelland

In the early 1500s, Portuguese, Basque and Norman fishermen began travelling to the Newfoundland. Many of them concentrated their efforts on a fishing ground just off a magnificent peninsula on the south coast of the Avalon Peninsula. The high headland with its vertical cliffs separated two wide bays. These religious fishermen named the cape that marked the end of the headland "Cabo de Sancta Maria," after the Patron Saint of Portugal, Mary the Virgin.

For one hundred and fifty years, they profited from the excellent herring and cod fishery off Cape St. Mary's each spring and summer. The French government began establishing colonies, first at Port Royal in Nova Scotia in 1606, and then in Quebec in 1608. They could not help but notice the expansion of English settlements along the northeastern coast of Newfoundland. An English stronghold on Newfoundland could effectively control the entrance of the Gulf of St. Lawrence threatening their own initiatives in North America. The French began developing a plan to stop the advance of the English in Newfoundland.

In 1662, King Louis XIV ordered his militia to establish a garrison on the south coast of the Avalon Peninsula. They chose an excellent site at the head of the largest bay near Cape St. Mary's. The place had been used by their countrymen as a summer fishing station for over a century. The site possessed a fine harbour, separated from the ocean by a long wide cobblestone beach. A narrow ocean inlet or *gut* was the only access to the harbour. Encircled by high hills, this fjord was large enough to hold one hundred and fifty fishing boats. The beach was ideal for drying the salted cod they caught off the Cape. They named the place *Plaisance*. This expression roughly translated refers to a summer harbour for pleasure boats - a marina of sorts. The name seems a bit ironic, given the importance that they assigned to access to the Newfoundland fishery.

The first of a series of fortifications was begun by thirty soldiers who landed with the colonists. It was a simple wooden structure built on a plateau just southeast across the arm from the village. With Plaisance only sixty miles overland from St. John's, tensions began to grow between the French fishermen and the West Country merchants on the English Shore. Raiders from St. John's made several attempts to destroy Plaisance in the latter part of the seventeenth century. In 1692, an English commodore named Williams made one particularly daring raid on Plaisance. That fall he entered the outer harbour at Plaisance with two 65 gun Ships-of-the-Line and three smaller frigates. He brought them into a battle line parallel to the beach and began firing broadsides into the poorly fortified village. After over two thousand salvos, the English ships departed leaving the place in a shambles.

After this attack, the French King, convinced that the English would soon try to overwhelm his little colony, ordered the construction of Fort Louis on the north side of the inlet. Its substantial earthen ramparts held twenty cannons, all trained on the entrance to the harbour. The Governor's house and the hospital were built behind the wooden palisade.

During the mid 1690s the fishery prospered. The little village across the gut on the stone beach grew to the size of a small town with several hundred inhabitants. They built simple wooden houses and wharfs along the edge of the South East Arm. A church, convent and school were also built there.

It was during this time that they began construction of two more fortifications on twin hilltops high above the town. With few funds from war ravaged France, construction progressed slowly on the main fort, known as the *Royal Redoubt*. The soldiers eventually erected a substantial stone rampart completely around the hilltop. Two stone-faced barracks, a powder magazine and several smaller sheds were built inside the walls. On the walls of the Royal Redoubt were located fourteen large cannons and two mortars which could easily sweep the outer harbour of Plaisance. A second smaller redoubt was built on an adjacent hilltop known as *Le Gaillardin*.

Beginning in 1701, with the outbreak of the War of the Spanish Succession, full scale hostilities broke out between the two fishing stations. Sieur d'Iberville and later Sieur de Subercasse used Plaisance as a base to successfully attack St. John's and harass English shipping all along the northeast coast of Newfoundland.

In the latter years of the War, the English managed to effectively blockade Plaisance from the sea. The French inhabitants were completely dependent on the supply ships from their homeland. Prevented from getting the desperately needed supplies, they experienced a disastrous series of famines. Prevented from gaining access to the sea to fish, the colonists began to leave Plaisance.

The war in Europe did not go well either. The French had been met with a series of defeats at the hands of the Austrians. In 1713, under the terms of the Treaty of Utrecht, they were forced to abandon all claims to Newfoundland. The French were expelled from Plaisance. Most fled to Louisbourg on Cape Breton Island. It was there that the French government built their last great fortress in North America. Their effort there was a continuation of their initial plan to use Plaisance as guardian of the entrance to the Gulf of St. Lawrence.

Fearing that the French may try to retake it, the British Admiralty were quick to take control of the area around Plaisance. They renamed the old town and the one hundred and fifty kilometre long bay beyond, *Placentia*. An English officer named Samuel Gledhill was appointed Governor of Placentia in 1719. He ruled Placentia with an iron fist. A treacherous and conniving fellow, Gledhill expropriated merchants' property in Placentia for his own benefit.

Before he was finally sacked in 1728, Gledhill left at least one intriguing legacy. Some time during his stay there, he had a naval chart prepared showing the layout of the town in relation to the inner harbour and the existing forts. He made clear reference to a *lighthouse* built beside what he called the *Old Castle*. This little known chart is the only reference ever made to the existence of a lighthouse on top of the *Old Castle*. The Royal Redoubt had been allowed to fall into ruin in the years following the expulsion of the French.

History records the construction of the first North American lighthouse in Boston harbour in 1716. The first Canadian lighthouse was built in Louisburg harbour in 1733 by the French. Could it be that Governor Gledhill ordered the construction of a lighthouse in Placentia

"A detail from the key in the Gledhill map."

harbour in the 1720s? If it ever existed, the lighthouse was likely a simple wooden tower with a fire set at its top. It would have been designed to act as a beacon for English ships attempting to enter the outer harbour.

After Count d'Haussonville's attack on St. John's in 1762, the English feared that the French would try to retake Placentia. They fortified both sides of the Gut in preparation of what appeared to be an imminent French attack. The ruins of the Royal Redoubt were repaired and named *Castle Graves* after the Governor of the day, Sir Thomas Graves. The English renamed the hilltop *Castlehill*. The attack never came and after the War of 1812 Placentia lost its prominence and became a quiet fishing village.

A number of West Country families established businesses there during those years after the expulsion of the French. It may have been their sense of kinship for the French that brought the first Irishmen to Placentia. Merchant families like the Sweetmans, the Saunders and the Walshes brought many Irish over to work in their fish stores, forges and boatyards. Throughout the remainder of the eighteenth century, and well into the nineteenth century, the Irish settled in Placentia and along the thirty mile stretch of rugged coastline south to Cape St. Mary's. Many were fleeing religious persecution and civil unrest in their homeland. Cruel penal laws were imposed on them by their English-controlled Parliament. The first of a series of potato famines devastated Ireland during this time.

Many of these Irish were attracted to the series of isolated river valleys indenting this shore. These steep-sided valleys met the sea in exposed coves. The land in the river valleys was fertile, so many turned to farming. The hard working immigrants, snug in their "green coves", began to provide farm produce for the markets in St. John's. The isolation of these communities gave them a haven to openly practice their Roman Catholic faith. They finally had an opportunity to make a better life. This isolation also meant that the Irish culture and language would be preserved there even to the present day.

By the mid nineteenth century, this part of the Avalon Peninsula became known as the *Cape Shores*. It was a thriving part of the Colony for the herring and cod fishery proved to be one of the best on the Island.

119

The popular expression "Cape St. Mary's pays for all" described the profitable fishery there. The saying meant that if your summer fishing did not go well on your home grounds, you could fish on the grounds off Cape St. Mary's. The fishery there was so rewarding that you would at least cover the costs of fishing that year.

The increasing trade and fishing activity meant that many fishing schooners and coastal boats had to pass the unlit and fog bound Cape St. Mary's. Many trans-atlantic steamers, lost in the dense fogs off the Cape, were drawn into Placentia Bay by the treacherous currents. Most were eastbound for Europe when they met their end. Inspector Oke had been attempting to light prominent Capes in succession south from St. John's. In 1857, the House of Assembly passed a Bill to erect a Lighthouse at Cape St. Mary's at his recommendation.

The following spring, Robert Oke began the difficult task of building the lighthouse at Cape St. Mary's. In his annual report, he wrote, "On the 26th June (1858), proceeded to Cape St. Mary's via Placentia, accompanied by the contractor, Mr. R.F. Sweetman; determined upon the site for the intended Light house. The site chosen is on the extreme point of the Cape; it is a flat table land, elevated above the level of the sea about three hundred feet. The light will command an uninterrupted range seaward as well as a considerable portion of St. Mary's and Placentia Bays." The foundations were laid that same summer for a brick tower. The decision to use brick would later haunt Robert Oke.

He had to make another difficult decision concerning the nature of the light mechanism. He wrote "...as there appears to be some difference of opinion as to whether a white fixed light, or a flashing red and white light, would be the best adapted for Cape St. Mary's, it may be well to place on record my reasons for preferring the latter description of light - and although a practical experience of twenty years would enable me to judge rightly, I have in the present instance, been a good deal guided by opinions gathered from unquestionable authorities on Light house Engineering, viz, Messrs. D. & T. Stevenson, Civil Engineers, Edinburgh, who for many years past have had charge of the Scotch Light houses." The Stevenson brothers began preparing a revolving catoptric mechanism of the first order. Twelve Argand lamps would produce alternately every minute a red and white light.

Oke had originally hoped to complete the project the following summer, but the site proved to be very inaccessible making it difficult to land construction materials. He explained to the House of Assembly the following year, "The difficulties attending the landing of materials, either at Cape Pine or Cape Race, are not to be compared with those which present themselves at Cape St. Mary's, and when it is recollected that the landing of the materials at Cape Race cost the Imperial Government nearly £800, and that a war steamer was engaged in that service two seasons at Cape Pine, the expense incurred at Cape St. Mary's, increased as it has been by vexatious delays consequent on an unusual prevalence of strong gales and bad weather, cannot be regarded otherwise that unavoidable."

The light mechanism was finally installed in the summer of 1860. The lighthouse was first put into operation on September 20, 1860. The total cost of the light house, complete with the mechanism, was £5491, nearly twice as much as Cape Race.

Two dwellings, one for the keeper, the other for his assistant, were built on each side of the brick tower. This detached arrangement was unique since most keeper's residences were semi-detatched, sharing a common wall. Each wood and clapboard structure was painted white with a red roof. They were attached to the lighthouse by covered walkways. John Reilly moved his family into the head keeper's residence in 1860. He was appointed as the first keeper at Cape St. Mary's.

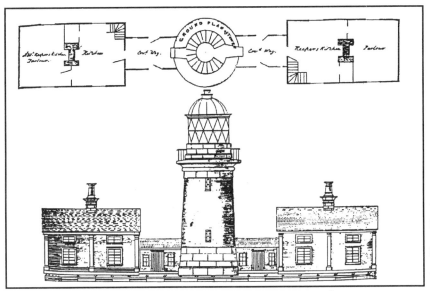

courtesy of Transport Canada

"Drawing, Cape St. Mary's Lighthouse with residences, 1860."

From the outset, the brick structure proved to be unsuitable for such an exposed site. The mortar between the bricks began to erode, softened by the driving salt spray that penetrated every crack and crevice. Before the decade had ended, the Lighthouse Service was forced to carry out a major renovation of the structure. They hired a contractor to re-pointed the tower "from foundation to the seat of the lantern". It was clear that unprotected masonry towers just could not work on the coasts of Newfoundland.

In 1877, a tragic series of events took place on the south coast of the Avalon Peninsula. Two sister ships, the SS *George Cromwell* and the SS

George Washington, were employed in carrying passengers between Halifax and St. John's. Both ships were well known, frequent visitors to St. John's harbour, making bi-weekly sailings, alternating with each other. The *George Cromwell* with twenty-six passengers and crew left Halifax in early January and simply disappeared. She was never heard from again. It is believed that she was wrecked six miles off Cape St. Mary's on a reef known as St. Mary's Cays. The actual wreck was never found. Portions of the ship turned up on a beautiful wide beach at Golden Bay, which lies just to the east of Cape St. Mary's. The scattered pieces of wreckage were burned, and there were several badly mutilated bodies. This fact led the investigators to speculate that as the ship struck the reef, the boilers exploded, burning the wreckage before it went down. Tragically, the *George Washington,* which left Halifax on the next sailing, was wrecked at Bristoe Cove seven miles from Cape Race only two weeks later with the loss of an additional thirty-one lives.

In 1881, after years of ill health, John Reilly retired and was replaced by William Collins. Thomas Young was his assistant keeper. It seems that they did not get along well from the start. In October of that year, Collins reported that his assistant had behaved improperly. Inspector Nevill sent out a replacement for Young, ordering him into St. John's to appear before the Board. While the Inspector never really explained what took place during that summer, it appears that William Collins was as much to blame for the incident as Thomas Young. Collins too was called before the Executive. In the end, it was reported, "After careful examination, the Board reprimanded both officers, cautioning them as to their future behaviour and ordering that the expenses of the inquiry should be paid by them."

The lighthouse structure continued to deteriorate; significant repairs were carried out in 1877 and in 1881. The lantern room floor was originally built of stone. The great weight of this platform so high atop the tower put extraordinary stress on the structure. In order to avoid serious damage it was replaced with a lighter cast iron system.

It was around this time that an amazing phenomenon began taking place on a sea stack just a mile southeast of the lighthouse. Thousands of great sea birds began to nest on the top of this three hundred foot high rock. They were gannets (*Morus brassanus*), magnificent birds with white streamlined bodies. They had chosen this isolated place as the site of their new nesting colony. It is believed that part of the huge gannet colony on the Funk Island had shifted to Cape St. Mary's in the early 1800s. Funk Island was the site of their original nesting colony. That tiny islet is located about one hundred miles off the northeast coast of Newfoundland. The gannets, about the size of a large goose, had been hunted for centuries by Newfoundland fishermen there. Even Jacques Cartier had landed on Funk Island in 1534 to take gannets for food.

Their graceful flight and amazing hunting technique proved to be an excellent diversion for the keepers and their families. An adult gannet's wing span is nearly six feet across. They developed the ability to glide for hours just above the ocean waves with only the occasional beat of those long, tapered wings. They were searching for caplin, herring and squid that swim in schools in Newfoundland waters in the spring

"Gannets"

and summer months. When a gannet spied its prey, it folded its long wings and plunged straight down into the sea in pursuit. The height of the dive and the great weight of the bird, drive it deep into the water. There they chase the silvery fish, swimming through the water with their webbed feet. If one bird is successful, other gannets, figuring there is a school, begin diving in the same area. It was and still is a spectacular sight for visitors to watch dozens of gannets hurtling from as high as a hundred feet straight into the sea.

Each March, thousands of gannets return from their winters sojourn off the southeastern coast of the United States. Their nests are nothing more than a mass of dried seaweed and debris. They return to the same ledge year after year. A single large white egg is laid in early June, the chicks hatch in early July. By late September, the gannetry is empty again as they head south to Florida.

The brick structure of the tower at Cape St. Mary's continued to deteriorate. The Lighthouse Service began to balk at the cost of its annual repair. In 1884, Inspector Nevill reported to the House of Assembly, "The brickwork of the tower is in very bad condition, the cement has peeled off in places showing rotten bricks beneath. The freestone base is also split and the stones are perishing. Work to arrest these evils somewhat will be needed; but the continued annual expenditure, together with the extensive and expensive repairs made on two occasions, and that are not effective for any length of time, make it a question of economy to do something that will be permanent. The only way that seems to do this is the casing of the whole of the masonry with iron. If this were once done the after estimate would only be on occasionally (a) coat of paint." This renovation was agreed to and the casing was prepared the following year at a cost of $2,000. In 1886, Inspector Nevill reported, apparently with great satisfaction, "The iron casing, backed as it is with concrete, makes a thoroughly safe building of one that has heretofore always been an annoyance."

It seems that the bad feelings between William Collins and Thomas Young continued throughout the 1880s. Finally, ten years after he had put them together, Nevill switched Young with Patrick Houlihan, the assistant keeper at Cape Pine. While Houlihan was getting on in years, he was an experienced keeper having worked for the Lighthouse Service for twenty-five years. When William Collins retired in 1898, Patrick Houlihan became the head keeper at Cape St. Mary's.

courtesy of Transport Canada

"Cape St. Mary's Lighthouse."

In 1906, a dramatic rescue took place in the surf of Golden Bay, just southeast of the lighthouse station. The little community of Golden Bay was really nothing more than a couple of fishermen's houses huddled on the back of the wide beach. It was located directly opposite one of the finest fishing grounds in the world.

Each fall, dozens of boats travelled the south coast of Newfoundland providing the folk of the little harbours and coves their winter supplies. They returned carrying the community's fish to markets in St. John's. The *Galatea* was one such boat, a little schooner, manned by four men. Her master was Captain Bond. In the fall, the ship and her crew were hired by the local merchant in Harbour Buffet. On December 14, the *Galatea* sailed out of St. John's harbour, her hold filled with all the Christmas trimmings, canned meats and cakes, children's toys, fine linens and the like for the families of the little south coast community. The little schooner met heavy seas off Cape Race and was forced to head for cover in Fermeuse to wait for the storm to blow over. A week later they finally departed, bound for Harbour Buffett.

Things did not go well for the little ship. Across from Cape St. Mary's, the main stays let go, and her forward mast came down. Captain Bond knew his little ship was done for. With the aft mast still up, he decided the best thing to do would be to bear her off downwind and head for Golden Bay. If the ship could make it, he would try to ground the *Galatea* on the beach. Hopefully he and his crew would make it to safety.

When Captain Bond could finally make out the beach, he knew that the *Galatea* would not last long in the maelstrom. There was an enormous surf on the beach that day, the huge Atlantic swells rolling up the shore pounded the coarse sand like a mighty fist. To make matters worse, the icy wind that howled through the halyards and stays of the remaining mast meant that they would freeze in minutes once they entered the water.

Mrs. Elsie MacDonald of Golden Bay stood looking out her kitchen window that morning. A strong woman, still young but hardened by the years of struggle to make a life for her husband and two teenage sons in that wild isolated place. Early that morning, her husband had taken his gun and headed out behind the village in hopes of shooting a rabbit or two to supplement their Christmas dinner.

Mrs. MacDonald couldn't believe her eyes when she saw the damaged schooner bearing straight into the Bay. Within minutes, the ship grounded some distance from shore. Immediately the surf began to break over the *Galatea*. The crew got the single lifeboat safely over the side and themselves into it. The great long swells threw the little dory before it. For a while it looked as though they would make it. As they neared the beach one great wave crashed into the boat, overturning it. They were all thrown into the icy sea. Without thinking of the consequences, Mrs. MacDonald dropped her dish towel and, flinging the door of her house open, dashed down onto the beach, her two sons right behind her.

By the time they reached the shore, Captain Bond and one of the crew actually managed to stumble frozen up onto the beach. Waving toward her house, she ordered them on toward the beckoning warmth of her kitchen. The other two crew did not fare so well. Not able to swim, they had decided to cling to the overturned dory. The huge waves carried the boat in each time, but as the waves receded, it would be pulled out again. Mrs. MacDonald knew the men were weakening as each moment passed. The three rescuers waded out into the surf. As the lifeboat came in with one big wave, Mrs. MacDonald and her two sons grabbed a line attached to the stern. They hung on as the wave drew back again. The effort was enough to ground the lifeboat. The two men staggered ashore into the arms of their rescuers. Not a moment too soon, for they all had begun to succumb to the icy water.

In a couple of minutes more they were all safely inside Mrs. Mac-Donald's little clapboard house. Captain Bond and his men stayed in Golden Bay until well past New Year's, housed comfortably by the residents, until their strength had been restored. The Christmas was a merry one too, for all the Christmas goodies meant for Harbour Buffett ended up high on the beach at Golden Bay.

Nothing remains of the little community of Golden Bay today except for the tops of a few stone foundations poking up amongst the long beach grass. The only residents are the large rafts of sea ducks which congregate there in the late fall.

In 1925, the old light mechanism was finally ready to give out, and a new mechanism housing a series of kerosene lamps was installed. During this period, a concrete casing was poured around the iron tower at Cape St. Mary's. This measure was intended to further strengthen the tower from the ravages of the severe weather there. In the 1920s Patrick Houlihan retired and James Conway took over. His son Arthur Conway replaced him in the 1930s. In the 1950s, the twin keepers' residences were replaced with a pair of single storey bungalows.

To get to Cape St. Mary's, you must take the Trans-Canada Highway to the turnoff for the Argentia Access Road. If you are coming from St. John's, this is a distance of about 90 km. Travel 45 km down this excellent highway, and turn left towards the Town of Placentia just before you get to the Marine Atlantic Ferry Terminus at Argentia.

A kilometre more, you will pass by Castlehill National Historic Site developed by Parks Canada. It is here in 1690s, that the French defenders of Plaisance built Fort Royale. From the top of the restored earthen and stone fort, you can get an excellent view of the Town and Placentia Bay. A modern Interpretive Centre has been constructed adjacent to the "Old Castle". If Gledhill's Lighthouse ever existed, it was constructed here.

Travelling on toward the Town of Placentia, you will notice the large steel bridge which spans the gut. On the near side, on the site presently occupied by a softball field, was the location of Fort Louis built by the French in 1691. Continue across the bridge and pass straight through the historic town of Placentia. To your left along the water's edge is where the French fishermen built their houses and their church. To the right lies the long stone beach, used for three hundred years to dry the salt cod.

From Placentia drive about 60 kilometres southeast along Route 100. The tour along the Cape Shore is spectacular. An excellent paved highway skirts along the coast, each turn opens a new wonderful vista. Watch out for stray sheep, for many of the residents still pasture their herds in meadows that lie along the road. The sheep have a penchant for warming themselves in the middle of the warm asphalt roadway.

The road rises and then falls straight down into a series of green coves. Each valley holds a different community. They have names like Cuslett, Patrick's Cove and Ship Cove. Some of these, like Gooseberry Cove, have been abandoned in the past twenty years.

The last community you must pass through is St. Bride's. Just 5 kilometres beyond St. Bride's, you should watch for a modest road turning off to the right; this will take you due south to Cape St. Mary's. If you miss the turn, you will end up in the community of Branch, the last town that makes up the Cape Shore.

The gravel road out to Cape St. Mary's has been recently replaced by a new asphalt one. For much of the sixteen kilometre drive, you will be heading south across a high, barren plateau. This part of the drive will take twenty minutes. You will know that you are nearly there when you reach a fairly steep ravine. Just take your time and you should have no problems. From beginning to end, it is about two hundred kilometres from downtown St. John's to Cape St. Mary's.

Park your vehicle in the area provided just outside of the white fence that surrounds the lighthouse station. The lighthouse is one hundred metres away at the very edge of the three hundred foot cliff which plunges straight into the sea. The tower is a bit of a disappointment. The twentieth century renovation has given the tower a squat, awkward shape. A new aluminum lantern sits on top, it houses a 400 Watt mercury vapour lamp. A simple bullseye lens focuses the light thirty miles out to sea. If you look carefully, the faint outline of the foundation of the keepers' residences can be seen below the short grass around the lighthouse tower. The fog alarm and a helicopter pad are located nearby. The two keepers' residences are still existent today. The first bungalow is still used as a residence for Vincent Keough, the present keeper at Cape St. Mary's. The other one houses an Interpretive Centre operated by the Wildlife Division.

Drop into the Centre, and get final directions to the Cape St. Mary's Ecological Reserve. The walk out to the vantage point will take you about a mile southeast of the lighthouse. Starting at the parking lot, strike out across the barrens. It is fairly easy going over the boggy ground, a waterproof pair of hiking boots would be helpful. **The route will at times take you close to the edge of the precipitous cliff. So mind your small children**. After ten minutes, on a clear day, you will see *Bird Rock* in the distance. It is a three hundred foot high sea stack which stands directly adjacent to the main body of the headland. Millions of years of erosion have worn away the softer stone that once connected the rock pinnacle to the rest of the cliff.

You can first recognise Bird Rock because it appears dazzling white against the black of the adjacent cliffs. As you approach, you will realize that the white rock is actually due to 5,000 nesting pairs of gannets.

They completely cover the top one third of the rock. This site is the second largest gannetry in North America after Bonaventure Island off the Gaspé Penninsula. It is a spectacular place. Watch these graceful birds as they hunt for caplin and other small fish in the sea. Dozens of birds at a time hurl themselves straight down from a great height to pursue the fish under water. This area is also an excellent place to see humpback whales feeding on the same fish.

Ten or fifteen more minutes will take you to the vantage point. The nesting gannets are only thirty metres away from where you stand, so try not to disturb them as you move around. **The cliff here drops straight down to a gravel beach three hundred feet below; there are no guard rails**. It is easy to see why these birds chose the site in the 1880s, for no natural predator can approach them.

Standing there you will realize that there are many more different kinds of seabirds nesting at Cape St. Mary's. Occupying the middle third of the cliffs that surround Bird Rock are the pretty little gulls know as kittiwakes (*Rissa tridactyla*). Their distinctive call originated their name. A bit smaller than a herring gull, they have a white head and body with a pearl grey back. Their *triangular* wing tips and legs are black, distinguishing them from other small gulls. Winter and summer, kittiwakes can be found far out to sea over much of eastern Atlantic waters. They are nimble in the air; constantly wheeling and turning on rapid wing beats, they are looking for small fish and shrimp on the surface of the ocean. Like other gulls, they are scavengers and can often be seen following fishing boats, chasing scraps of fish thrown out by the fishermen.

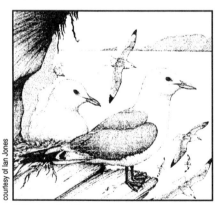

courtesy of Ian Jones

"Kittiwakes"

Cape St. Mary's is one of their largest nesting colonies. There are other colonies on Baccalieu Island and on the islands off Witless Bay, south of St. John's. They nest in the cracks and crevasses of the sheer rock face. A simple nest of dried seaweed is constructed to hold two buff coloured eggs. These will hatch after three and a half weeks. The young are cared for by their parents. By late July they are old enough to make their first flight off the cliff and fend for themselves.

Standing at the edge of the precipice, peer down to the lower ledges of the cliffs. There you will see some of the 12,000 pairs of common murres (*Uria aalgee*) nesting. These murres are the last of the three main residents of Cape St. Mary's. Known locally as *turrs*, they are

"Murres, Razor-bills and Thick-billed Murres."

members of the alcid or auk family. About the size of a small duck, they are taken in large numbers as a traditional winter fare in many Newfoundland kitchens. They are easily recognized as their heads and upper parts of their bodies and wings are a dark grey-brown. The lower parts of their bodies are white. Their black bills are long and tapered, which distinguishes them from their near cousins, the thick-billed murre (*Uria lomvia*).

Their bodies have adapted well for their life swimming on and under the ocean. They spend nearly their entire lives far out to sea, coming to land only to rear their young. They feed on small fish which they hunt by diving. When they dive they use their short wings to propel themselves through the water. While this characteristic allows them to pursue their prey as deep as three hundred feet, their short wings mean that they have an amusing awkward way of flying. Much the same as the puffins, the murres' wings must beat at a very fast rate in order to get themselves airborne. With short tails, they do not manoeuvre well. Landing on the narrow ledges at Cape St. Mary's would be an amusing affair if it weren't for the fact that often their eggs are dislodged and lost in the cliffs.

On land, they look like miniature penguins for their blackish legs are located way back on their bodies. They must waddle and flap along, then they move around their nesting site. The murres do not build a nest; rather, they lay their single large egg right on the rock shelf. The adults take turns keeping their egg warm until the chick hatches in about four weeks. The adults feed the chicks huge quantities of the silvery caplin so plentiful in the waters below. Amazingly, three weeks after hatching, the half grown chicks are ready to make the plunge off

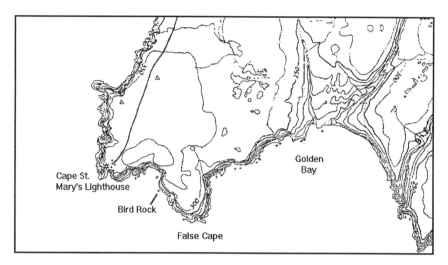

Cape St. Mary's Lighthouse

Bird Rock

Golden Bay

False Cape

the cliffs. They escape out to sea where they learn to hunt for themselves and grow to full size. Cape St. Mary's is just one of several nesting colonies in Newfoundland. There are other large colonies on Funk Island and on the islands off Witless Bay.

Including the gannets, kittiwakes and murres, there are over 50,000 birds nesting in a very restricted area. This figure does not include smaller numbers of northern razor-bills, black guillemots and herring gulls that nest here. At the height of the summer the bird sanctuary is a noisy, raucous place. Hundreds and hundreds of birds are in motion at any one time. Standing on the vantage point you cannot help but notice that the bracing salt air has been replaced by a very powerful odour of a different kind. Carefully walk around the edge of the cliffs until you are opposite the vantage point. It you continue on there is a path which will take you to False Cape. From there you can look east to Golden Bay.

Looking northwest with Bird Rock in the foreground, you can see the regular flash of the light at Cape St. Mary's in the distance. It is a truly remarkable place, a sight that cannot be missed if you are travelling on the south coast of the Avalon Peninsula.

Ferryland Head
(Flash 4 sec.; eclipse 4 sec.; flash 18 sec.)
Calvert's Light

"...the coldest harbour of the Land,
where those furious Windes and Icy Mountaynes doe play,
and beate the greatest part of the Yeare....."
　　　　　　　from William Vaughan's *Newlanders Cure*, 1630

We must accept that the earliest English efforts to colonize North America were not made by the Kings and Queens of Britain. Rather, they were made by practical businessmen who knew that there were lucrative markets for the furs, timber and the codfish so plentiful in the New World.

In the first decade of the seventeenth century, investors from a number of English port cities began forming private companies. These companies were authorized by Royal Charter, and gave the subscribers a sole control over huge tracts of land and coastline. They were entrepreneurs; they hoped that they could finance the costs of establishing a colony by pooling their money.

There were several notable examples of this type of proprietary colonization. Sir Walter Raleigh's ill-fated colony at Roanoke Island, Virginia was the first, in 1584. Twenty-three years later, the second Virginia Company was successfully established at Jamestown. By the

1630's, the first great migration of English settlers flooded into New England.

In 1610, just three years after the founding of the second Virginia Company, a group of merchants in London and Bristol formed the *Newfoundland Company*. These men were familiar with the profitable fishery off the east coast of Newfoundland. They believed that a monopoly over the activities of the whole of the Island could mean great riches. By establishing a Newfoundland base, they hoped to dominate the fishery there, ensuring a steady supply of salt cod to send back to England.

One of the investors was Captain John Guy; he was appointed Governor by his peers. Captain Guy established the first Newfoundland plantation at Cupers (Cupids) Cove in Conception Bay. Unfortunately the colony had its share of problems. It was under constant attack by the pirate Peter Easton. The soil was poor, and the winters were long and cold. As investment dried up, many of the original shareholders back in England began feuding amongst themselves.

By the fifth year, the colony began encountering financial problems. In order to refinance their operation, the officers of the Company decided to sub-divide their holdings. They sold a huge portion of the southern part of the peninsula to a rich Welshman named William Vaughan. A couple of years later, facing similar financial problems, Vaughan chose to sell small slices of his holdings to two new investors. The first investor was Sir Henry Cary (later Lord Falkland); he received a narrow piece of land which ran between harbours in Aquaforte and Fermeuse on the Southern Shore.

A second tract lay just to the north of Falkland's property. It was centered on the harbour at Ferryland. The land was sold to Sir George Calvert in 1620. For many years, George Calvert had been the Secretary of State to King James I. Given the numerous intrigues and plots against James I during his reign, a faithful Secretary of State was definitely an asset. These were the years of great turmoil which followed the English Reformation in 1534. The practice of Catholicism was out of favour in the Protestant Court of James I. English Catholics were subjected to a form of religious persecution. While Calvert was raised a Protestant, he would soon convert to the Catholicism. Historians believe that this was the main reason for Calvert's purchase of the property in Newfoundland, he intended to establish a sanctuary for English Catholics there.

Ferryland was situated thirty-two miles south of St. John's by sea. Throughout the previous century, it had been used as a summer fishing station by all the marine nations of Europe. The place was within easy access of excellent fishing grounds and a dense boreal forest covered the rolling hills behind the harbour.

Ferryland also possessed a superb harbour. A high rock headland protected the whole of the harbour's south side. This headland was connected to the land by a narrow isthmus known locally as *the Downs*. The name *Ferryland* is probably a veiled reference to this distinctive headland. The name is believed to have been derived from the English corruption of the French word *Forillon*. This is the name the French and the Portuguese gave the place in the sixteenth century. It means a high rock lying near shore which has become separated from the land by the erosion of the sea.

The harbour is further sheltered by a large island which lies just to the northeast. This provided Ferryland with needed protection from the northeasterlies which bore down in the winter months. The French called it *Isle de Bois* or woody island. This is curious for today Bois Island is covered in long green grass, not a tree remains to be seen.

One final feature made Ferryland harbour unique. A crescent shaped breakwater of gravel and stones, deposited eons ago by some glacier, created a small, very protected inner harbour. This nearly landlocked anchorage was known as *the Pool*. It was here that Calvert's first few settlers landed in the summer of 1621. They were under the command of Captain Edward Wynne. His first order was to build a "mansion house" for the Governor. This was a large one-and-a-half storey stone structure. It was forty-four feet long and fifteen feet wide. The residence was built at the very edge of the inner harbour. A variety of workshops, forge and store rooms were also constructed that first winter. They even built a simple wooden palisade around the settlement to protect against marauding French privateers.

With Calvert's support, more settlers were sent the following year and the colony prospered. Calvert was so encouraged that he decided to try to get control over more land on the peninsula. In 1623, he persuaded James I to give him a Royal Charter to an expanded colony. Calvert called it *Avalonia*. Perhaps he was remembering the Avalon of old. It was there in Somerset where legend placed the founding of English Christianity by Joseph of Arimathea. This illusion was very likely on his mind, because two years later, he resigned his position in the High Court and became a Roman Catholic. In recognition of the years of service, the King gave him the title of Lord Baltimore.

Filled with enthusiasm, Lord Baltimore (Calvert) and his family sailed for Ferryland to begin a new life. He brought with him two Catholic priests, who offered the first Roman Catholic mass in British North America when they arrived. Unfortunately, things did not work out for the new Lord Baltimore. The French privateer, the Marquis de la Rade with three ships and four hundred men, began harassing Calvert's operation. Matters grew worse, as the colony had to suffer through two dreadful winters. Many of Baltimore's settlers died of malnutrition. By 1629, Lord Baltimore and his wife had enough. He decided to move his colony to the more temperate lands of Virginia. There he established a new colony, calling it *Maryland*. The City of Baltimore bears his name today.

While Lord Baltimore left with his family and servants, many of the fishermen decided to stay. Eight years later, the Cavalier, David Kirke, sailed into Ferryland harbour to take control of the settlement. Kirke was an English pirate, who had been in the service of the new English King, Charles I. He and his band successfully captured Quebec City in 1629. As a reward, he was made the Governor of the Colony of Avalon. At the same time, the Colony was granted its own Coat of Arms. It was based on the St. George's Cross with two Lions and two Unicorns located alternating in each corner. This is the same Coat of Arms which was adopted by the Newfoundland Government in 1927 and is still used today.

David Kirke lived in Ferryland with his family for several years. He fortified the strategically located Bois Island. Kirke even considered inviting King Charles I to flee England for Ferryland with the rise in the power of Oliver Cromwell. Charles was eventually beheaded and Kirke was forced to return to England to defend a dispute of claim made by Baltimore's descendants over ownership of Ferryland.

Despite the controversy over who owned the harbour and even with devastating attacks by the Dutch in 1673 and the French in 1694 and 1705, English merchants and their Irish servants continued to use Ferryland as their base to pursue the fishery. The community grew to be one of the largest settlements found along the "English Shore". After the French attack in 1762, a substantial fort was built on Bois Island, together with several batteries on Ferryland Head and the Downs. Still more fortifications were built to defend against American privateers during the War of 1812.

With the peace, the people of Ferryland returned to their peaceful co-existence beside the sea. The fishery prospered and local merchants developed a brisk trade in salt fish with the great merchantile families of St. John's. With this increased local trade, coastal traffic grew between Ferryland and St. John's.

The need for effective communications between Newfoundland, the Maritimes and the New England States increased after the War of 1812. In the years that followed, fast ships were contracted by the Government to travel between St. John's and Halifax carrying the Royal Mails and freight. The swift Mail Steamer *Falcon* was one such ship. For several years in the late 1840's, she travelled regularly between Newfoundland and Nova Scotia. She was owned by Baine, Johnston and Company.

On the evening of May 7, 1851, Captain George Corbin ordered his men to slip her lines and ease the *Falcon* away from the Queen's Wharf in St. John's harbour. That night, as the *Falcon* met the open sea off the Cape Spear lighthouse, Captain Corbin altered the steamer's course to the south. This passage was one with which Corbin had become very familiar, having travelled it many times before in all kinds of weather. Little did he know that the compass that they used to steer her had been damaged during the ship's most recent layover in St. John's. Driving southward, the *Falcon* was quickly enveloped in a thick sea fog.

Five hours after leaving St. John's, at 2 o'clock in the morning, the *Falcon* was off Ferryland Head. Blinded in the fog, she steamed straight into a reef on the north side of Bois Island. Believing that their course was properly set, they must have been going full out when she struck. The bottom of the steamer ripped open and she began sinking quickly. The passengers and crew managed to clamber onto the island with the precious mail bags and little else. They spent a cold night there on the abandoned island. In the morning, they were picked up by residents of Ferryland and returned to St. John's.

Several other shipwrecks took place in and around Ferryland harbour in the 1850's, most notably the schooner *Margaret* and the *Hammer*. These accidents drew the attention of the Colony's Lighthouse Service. They considered establishing a station along the sixty mile stretch of rugged coastline that extends from Cape Spear to Cape Race. Ferryland Head posed a particular hazard, for it jutted out from the coast like a pointed dagger.

In the spring of 1859, the House of Assembly enacted a bill "to provide for the erection of a Lighthouse on Ferryland Head." Strangely, it would be another ten years before the Service actually began the process of building a lighthouse there. In July of 1869, Inspector Oke and his protégé, John Nevill, travelled to Ferryland to select the site for the station. They chose the highest point of land on the very tip of the headland. The lighthouse and a duplex residence for the keepers were probably designed by Nevill. Unfortunately, it was still too early for them to learn their lesson at Cape St. Mary's. Nevill specified that the tower was to be built of brick. The project was awarded to William Cambell and Thomas Burridge, two well-known masons from St. John's. Work began in the following spring. Interestingly, both James and Dennis Cantwell from the Cape Spear station were sent out that summer to help oversee the initial construction of the tower.

The lighthouse at Ferryland Head was intended to be a coastal light rather than a landfall light. It was to exhibit a fixed white light, illuminated by a system of double wick concentric kerosene lamps. The fixed rather than revolving nature of this light meant that the vertical framing bars for the glass in the lantern would obscure too much of the light. Nevill chose to use a helical arrangement. He reasoned that the inclined bars crossing the fixed gaze of the light would have minimal effect. The light mechanism was designed by the engineering firm of D & T Stevenson Limited and built by Chance Brothers of Birmingham, England. The final work was not completed until 1871, when the dioptric light mechanism was installed.

Thirty-six-year-old Michael Kearney was appointed as the first keeper at Ferryland Head. He would be keeper for eleven years. During this time, it seems that he would cause Inspector Nevill considerable grief over his actions. His first assistant was William Costello. The problems started in March, 1875, when the light was reported out during Costello's watch. Inspector Nevill investigated and subsequently removed Costello to Cape Pine, placed under the experienced eye of George Hewitt. Michael Kearney was kept on at Ferryland Head.

An Irishman named Patrick Keough was hired as his new assistant. Keough had been blessed with a large family. When they joined the station's staff, they already had one set of twins together with several other children. His wife, Ellen, would deliver another pair of twins soon after moving into the lighthouse residence. The happy sounds of children's laughter must have rung across the high rock barren upon which the lighthouse was built.

Unfortunately, Kearney didn't get along well with Keough either. This must have been disappointing for Inspector Nevill considering the racket that took place between the Kearney and Costello the year before. Nevill would write in his annual report, "A state of ill-feeling and disagreement between the keepers was shown which boded ill for efficient working".

During these early years after the lighthouse had been built, the staff began noticing another problem. The brick face of the lighthouse had begun to deteriorate. In 1877, the original contractor, Thomas Burridge, was called back to undertake major repairs to the tower.

The following year, tragedy struck the lighthouse station at Ferryland Head. It was a misery which was common in those days before the discovery of powerful antibiotics. It was an event which struck swiftly and which devastated Patrick Keough's family. That fall, in a period of no more than eleven days, an outbreak of diphtheria would first take the two older twins, and then a week later, the two younger twins. They were all buried together in the small Roman Catholic cemetery overlooking the Ferryland harbour. Inspector Nevill concluded that "the extremely small rooms and limited accommodation at this station had been a predisposing cause of the disease." Despite his comments, it would be another eight years before Nevill would recommend a major expansion of the keeper's residence at Ferryland Head.

The brick tower continued to deteriorate. Nevill wrote, "Every year, new cracks show themselves in the brick of the light tower, and seem of quite a mysterious character. If there were extensive settlements in the

"The Pool and the Downs by WR MacAskill."

work, or failure of the foundations or rupture of the work laterally by frost, they could be understood, but none of these are apparent and still the bricks break across - a brick here and a brick there and they have to be cut out and replaced by sound ones to keep out the weather....the bricks are very much shattered, and there is no apparent reason for their failure, as the bricks were good and very carefully selected, and the masonry was well done."

Beyond the condition of the tower, Nevill was getting distressing reports from ship captains travelling the Southern Shore. He wrote "Rumours come to me from time to time that this light is neglected to the extent of having been out seemingly on more than one occasion. These are but rumours, and I cannot obtain facts to verify them, but I know that the bad feelings existing between the keeper and assistant (mutual I believe) are having a bad effect on the station."

Finally, a year later, Nevill found himself in a position where he could take some action. He reported, "In April last (1882), the assistant keeper made a formal complaint as to the conduct of the keeper, accompanied by specific charges of serious neglect of duty." An inquiry was held in St. John's and forty-seven year old Michael Kearney was "retired". William Costello, the same keeper who had been sent to Cape Pine seven years before, was returned to Ferryland Head as the head keeper.

For all the sad memories associated with the loss of his children and the bitter arguments with Kearney, it is surprising that Patrick Keough would decide to stay on as the assistant keeper. It was very fortunate though, as Patrick Keough would be involved with a spectacular rescue the following year.

On August 3, 1883, the splendid four masted barquentine, *Octavia*, sailed from Sydney harbour bound for St. John's. This ship was also owned by Baine, Johnston and Company. She carried Cape Breton coal for the market in Newfoundland. A good wind filled her square rigged sails, allowing Captain Disney and his crew to bring the *Octavia* to with in sight of the southern coast of the Avalon Peninsula by the next evening. There the wind began to drop and a dense fog set in. At 8 pm, she lay becalmed only a mile off Ferryland Head. As darkness settled on the ocean, the crew grew fearful. They found that the *Octavia* was being drawn ashore by a strong inward current. She was slowly being pulled onto the rocks there below the lighthouse. When she struck the jagged reef, heavy ocean swells began pounding the ship. She started to break up immediately.

Alerted by distress flares, Costello and Keough were waiting above on the cliff. They threw a lead and line across to the stricken vessel. A stout rope was pulled back and secured to a rock outcrop on shore. Then, one by one, the crew of the *Octavia* made that tenuous trip to shore. They had to drag themselves through the sea that broke between the ship and the shore. Finally, it was the last man's turn, he was the second mate. Half way across, the rope parted, and he fell into the sea. Without waiting a moment, Keough tied a line around his waist and dove into the white water. Intent on the drowning man lost in the dark, Keough had to swim between the spars and masts of the wrecked ship before finally reaching him. Costello and the ship's crew then pulled them both safely back to shore.

Patrick Keough was recognized for the heroism that he showed that August night. Sir Frederick Carter, the Prime Minister, presented him a Silver Medal for Bravery on behalf of the Royal Humane Society.

The tower continued to deteriorate for another ten years. Finally in 1892, a contract was let to encase the lighthouse in iron sheathing. Nevill argued, "The only effectual (solution) would be to case the tower with iron, backed with concrete in a similar manner to work done at Cape St. Mary's. This would make the building practically indestructible, requiring but paint for its future annual maintenance". He was right, for one hundred years after this work was completed, the tower is still in fine shape.

In December 1903, another tragedy took place at Ferryland Head. The eighty ton Danish schooner *Sigrid* went ashore in an early winter storm. Captain Petersen was experienced in Newfoundland waters as he had freighted codfish to Oporto, Spain for many years. That December, the *Sigrid* was returning to Newfoundland in ballast when she met her icy end. In the darkness of that stormy night, she struck the sheer cliff face at Ferryland Head. The five crew never had a chance, for the schooner broke up immediately. When their bodies finally washed ashore, they had been horribly mutilated by the ravages of the sea.

"Ferryland Head Lighthouse, 1910."

Two years later, William Costello died at the station after more than thirty years of service. His son, John, became the new head keeper at the Ferryland Head Lighthouse. John Costello had worked beside his father for twelve years after Philip Keough passed away. John's younger brother, Gus, became the assistant keeper. John's twenty- year steward-ship of the lighthouse would pass quietly away. Several shipwrecks took place off Ferryland Head during these years, prompting a number of calls to construct a fog alarm on the headland. A minor fire in the lantern in 1919 caused sufficient damage to force the replacement of the lens and lamps with a new mechanism. This one was also built by Chance Brothers and was installed in 1921. This light mechanism still operates in the tower today.

The new light was not enough to keep the SS *Torhamvan* off the reef at Coldeast Point in 1926. This 3400 ton cargo ship was owned by the Lakefield Steamship Line. At 1 pm, on October 29, 1926, she left St. John's bound for Halifax and Montreal loaded with general cargo. There was an extremely dense fog that evening, so the Captain ordered his ship to reduce her speed as they travelled southward towards Cape Race. Somehow, the currents managed to draw the ship off course. By 6 pm she had strayed into the shallow water between Bois Island and Goose Island which lay just to the north. The inhabitants of Ferryland could hear the rending of steel as the captain attempted to manoeuvre the great steamer over the reefs. Eventually, the heavy sea drove her high up on the beach at Coldeast Point on the north side of the harbour. The sea was so heavy that it would take most of the night for the rescue of the crew by the residents. The SS *Torhamvan* was a complete loss. Within a few years the hull of the freighter was smashed and rusted by the sea. Today, all that is left of the *Torhamvan* are hulking remains of its boilers.

"Ferryland Head Lighthouse"

John Costello died in November 1927 at fifty-one years. His brother, Gus, became the fourth keeper at Ferryland Head Lighthouse. He operated the station throughout the 1930's, retiring in 1939 at age sixty years. His son, William, or Billy as he was known locally, became the last keeper to be responsible for the lighthouse at Ferryland Head. Billy Costello operated the light until he retired in 1970.

The Canadian Coast Guard made the facility automatic that year. They replaced the kerosene lamps with a single 500 W quartz-iodine lamp triggered by a photocell. The Coast Guard administration had planned to demolish the one-hundred-year-old structure. The Ferryland Historical Society saved the lighthouse from destruction when they persuaded the Minister of Transportation, the late Hon. Don Jamieson, to intervene. Eventually the Historical Society gained control of the site. The Newfoundland artist Gerry Squires was attracted to the site by its wild beauty and isolation. He lived in the lighthouse during the 1970's, leasing it from the Historical Society for five dollars per year. Squires used the keeper's residence as a studio to create many of his early paintings. He departed in the 1980's, moving to Holyrood to continue his painting. The lighthouse residence is abandoned now. While it is still standing, it has been completely gutted by vandals.

140

To travel to Ferryland Head Lighthouse, you will travel the same route that you took to reach Cape Race and Cape Pine. You must head through the west end of St. John's, taking the Southern Shore Highway (Route 10) southward. Drive through picturesque arms of the sea, cut by glaciers tens of millions of years ago. Huge quantities of gravel and cobble stone were washed down the glacial rivers, only to be thrown back up by the sea to form barachois or great cobble beaches at the head of many of these narrow bays. In the sixteenth and seventeenth centuries, the English settled in the comfortable harbours. For four hundred years, fishermen have turned their fishing boats towards the golden sun in the east to fish on the incredibly rich fishing grounds that lie just offshore. Drive through historic towns such as Bay Bulls, Witless Bay, Cape Broyle and Calvert. Each possesses its own excellent harbour formed eons ago by the glaciers.

It's about eighty kilometres from downtown St. John's to Ferryland. The drive takes about one hour. As you come around the last big turn just past the turnoff for the community of Calvert, you will see a beautiful view of Calvert Bay with Bois Island and the Ferryland Head stretching out before you. You should just make out the old lighthouse tower on the top of the distant point.

Drive along the coastal highway, watching for the old Holy Trinity Church on your right. This is one of the oldest Catholic churches in Newfoundland, its cornerstone was laid in 1863. The stone was quarried on Bois Island. At the Church, turn left onto the side road that drops down toward the water and *Bernard Kavanagh's* warehouse. Drive another five hundred metres to reach the site of Lord Baltimore's original settlement beside *the Pool*. Take some time to explore this beautiful, quiet place. This small lagoon is about seventy-five metres across. Usually it is full of fishermen's boats tied up to rickety wooden wharfs in much the same way as in Lord Baltimore's time.

Starting in 1985, the archaeologist Jim Tulk with other colleagues from Memorial University, began excavations on this site. They were searching for the "mansion house" built by Captain Wynne in the winter of 1621. They found a complex series of massive stone foundations together with considerable quantities of earthenware and glassware. These artifacts have been tentatively dated to the mid seventeenth century. They discovered what appears to be a simple forge built into the hill across the road. Divers discovered a sixty-foot-long *Sack boat* submerged in ten feet of water at the bottom of the Pool. These small sailing boats were used to carry colonists and supplies to the settlement in the spring and salt cod back to England each fall. Dr. Tulk received new funding in 1992 to continue his efforts with his students in exploring Lord Baltimore's settlement. A small steel building was constructed to preserve the artifacts as they are retrieved from the dig. One of the workers would be glad to show you around this makeshift labratory.

Those with a faint heart may wish to leave their cars in the small parking lot provided beside the edge of the Pool. It is about two kilometres out to the lighthouse. Between two fishermen's houses, you should notice a narrow rocky road that heads out across the Downs. There is a small sign erected at the beginning of the "Lighthouse Road". This road is passable but it is steep and washed out with a large rut running down its centre. It you are not careful, the road is quite capable of taking off your muffler. The gravel road runs along the north side of Ferryland Head, passing fenced green pastures where for three hundred years grazed the residents' cattle. They are abandoned now, left to the herring gulls and the red fox.

About half way out this road, in the tall green grass, you will notice a large eighteenth century cannon abandoned beside the road on the left hand side. If you are still in your car this is a good place to park it, for just ahead lies the most difficult part of the road. From this vantage, you can look across to grassy Bois Island just offshore. It was here that a series of forts were built. The French and Dutch made numerous attacks on Ferryland. You can almost imagine the dazzling white sails of the enemy frigates and the crack of the twenty pounders returning fire from the batteries buried on the island.

From here it is another kilometre to the lighthouse, only a short distance to walk. The land narrows here to form an isthmus connecting the main part of the peninsula to the actual cape. There is a steep bank on each side of the road running down to the sea. If you are still in your car, you will need quite a run to get up the hill on the other side of the isthmus. **The road is very narrow and the sides are steep so it is recommended that you leave your car in the meadow across from the abandoned canon**. On the hill on the other side of the isthmus, the English built a small battery to defend against American privateers during the War of 1812.

The last kilometre of road is level and quite passable. There are frequent deep pot-holes (usually filled with water), with lots of sharp boulders sticking out of the gravel. The boots that you wear will prove quite handy as you skirt around some of the larger puddles. It is about two-and-one-half kilometres from the turnoff at the highway and the Ferryland Head Lighthouse.

The lighthouse together with the attached residence is perched on a rocky outcrop overlooking Calvert Bay. The cast iron tower rises solidly from the rock, its bolts showing a hundred and twenty years of red paint. The rotating light can be seen through the helical glazing of the lantern, originally proposed by John Nevill in 1870.

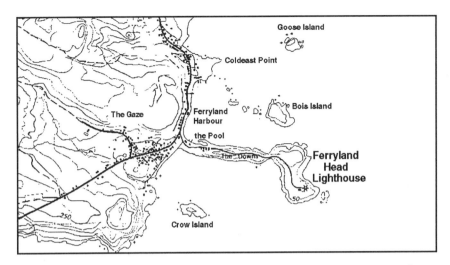

The keeper's residence still stands on a beautifully cut stone foundation. It is a two-storey structure with a curious doubled plan, designed to accommodate the two keepers' families. The twin stairs, several narrow coal grates and large fireplaces remain. The residence is sheathed in a heavy wooden plank which gave the house extra strength in the high winter winds. Heavy timbers can be observed supporting the second floor and the roof. Only a shell remains of the house. It has been grossly vandalized, the windows are gone and most of the interior is demolished. Traces of Victorian wallpaper and old newspapers can still be seen pasted to the wall. They hang in tatters now.

Stand at one of the north windows looking back across the field that once contained a flourishing garden. You can see Calvert Bay in the distance, you can almost hear the sounds of the children's laughter that rang there so many years ago.

Cape Ray
(Flash 1 second; eclipse 14 seconds)
The Gulf Light

".... we today walked round Cape Ray, here leaving the French Shore and entering upon American Newfoundland, or that division of the coast on which the Americans have a right of fishing and of drying their fish. On the shore north of Cape Ray lay several wrecks of ships and their cargos of timber..... The high lands of Cape Ray lie several miles inland, north-east of the Cape, and consist of a group of granite mountains seemingly nearly two thousand feet in height. The scenery among them is sublime; the steep sides of the wedge-shaped valleys appear smooth and striped at a distance, owing to the crumbled rocks and blocks detached by frost being hurled from the very summits to the bottom, where they lie in heaps of ruins."
from *the Journal of William E. Cormack*, November 29, 1822

Looking at a map of Newfoundland, a casual observer may notice the strong triangular shape of the Island. Much of the early lighthouse development in Newfoundland occurred along the leading southeastern point of this triangle. The station at Cape Race was recognized early on as a "landfall" lighthouse. Cape Pine, Ferryland Head and Cape St. Mary's stations were all located in the vicinity of that same southeastern point of the triangle. Together they played a significant role in the marine history of the province.

What of the lighthouses on the other two points of the triangle? Cape Norman on the tip of the Northern Peninsula, together with Point Amour and the two lighthouses on Belle Isle guarded the northern passage through the Strait of Belle Isle. An account of what happened at Cape Norman follows in the next chapter.

The final point of the triangle is formed by a low, rocky headland that juts out into the Gulf of St. Lawrence. Known as Cape Ray, it is located on the very southwestern tip of the Island. The name Cape *Ray* probably came from the same origin as Cape *Race*. They were derived from the Breton term *rasum* which means *to shave*. The broad headland posed a considerable obstacle to the early mariners attempting to pass between the Gulf and the Atlantic Ocean. Tacking their sailing ships back and forth, it was said that they would *shave* past the Cape in order to get free wind.

The story of Cape Ray begins much earlier than the visits by Basques fishermen. We must look back hundreds of millions of years to when the face of our planet looked much different. Cape Ray is situated on one of the most important geological sites in the province. Three different geological zones together with their fault lines pass either under Cape Ray or close by.

In order to understand what happened there, we must first consider the Theory of Plate Tectonics first proposed by Dr. Tuzo Wilson of the University of Toronto. He suggested that continent-sized plates literally float on the liquid core of the planet. These huge pieces of the earth's crust are set into slow motion by the cooling action of the molten magma. Geologists have been able to support the theory by measuring the movement of the plates as they rift or spread apart. They have shown that the Atlantic Ocean is still widening along the Mid-Atlantic Ridge, creating a new ocean bottom each year. Conversely, continental plates grind past each other, along a *fault line*, each plate moving in an opposite direction. The violent earthquakes along the San Andreas Fault in California are an example of continental plates in motion.

Dr. Wilson suggested that two "super" continents existed five hundred million years ago. They were composed of numerous plates which would eventually separate and reform into the continents that we know today. The first super continent was named *Laurentia*; it contained the ancient *Canadian Shield*. Today, this one billion year old geological structure forms more than half the land mass of Canada. A portion of the Canadian Shield extends into Newfoundland. It runs from the Cape Norman at the very tip of the Northern Peninsula, south to Deer Lake, and then southwest to Cape Ray. Geologists attempting to classify the geological structures in Newfoundland call this region the Humber Zone. This is the first of four geological zones that make up the Island.

A wide, shallow sea separated Laurentia from *Gondwanaland*, the other super continent. The *Iapetus Ocean*, as it was named, teamed with primitive marine life. Over millions of years, this tropical ocean became covered with various sediments, sands and the calcified shells of early invertebrate creatures. The sediments deposited onto the continental shelves that surrounded the ancient continents.

About 475 million years ago, the continents began to drift together. For seventy-five million years, they drew closer, slowly crushing the Iapetus Ocean bottom. Fractures opened up, and a myriad of volcanic islands formed in the shrinking ocean. Most of the seabed was pulled down below the earth's crust. A small portion of the ancient ocean bottom remains. Starting at Cape Ray the formation runs for a hundred kilometres off to the northeast along the Cabot Fault then continues on through to Central Newfoundland ending on the northeast coast. Geologists named this geological structure the Dunnage Zone.

Eventually, the continents collided all along what would become the eastern seaboard of North America. The crushed ocean bed rafted high up over the Laurentian continent. Molten granite squeezed through the fractures in the crust, into space that formed beneath this sedimentary rock. A great North American mountain system was created by this action. The Appalachian Range runs from the West Coast of Newfoundland through the Gaspe Peninsula on to New England. It continues as far as the State of Alabama. These majestically high mountain peaks were comparable in height to the Canadian Rockies. Four hundred million years of weathering have worn them down to the more modest series of ranges we know today. The remnants of the Appalachian Mountains in Newfoundland still retain some of that majesty. They are known as the Long Range Mountains.

After the collision, the two continents stayed "glued" together for two hundred million years. Then during the early Jurassic period, two new continents began moving apart, creating the Atlantic Ocean between them. The split took place to the east of the old ocean bed. Geologists believe that portions of Gondwanaland were left "stuck" to the newly formed North American continent. The first piece was a narrow band of sedimentary rock, that had been part of its continental shelf. This formation was left incredibly deformed and changed by the collision. The Gander Zone, as it is called, runs from Cape Ray, along the South Coast then turns up through Gander to the northeast coast in the area of the Eastport Peninsula.

The second part of Gondwanaland was actually a piece of the original land mass. It has similar characteristics to rock formations on the west coast of Africa. Today, it forms what we know to be the Burin, Bonavista and Avalon Peninsulas. This region is called the Avalon Zone.

Three of the four geological zones of Newfoundland pass each other in the vicinity of Cape Ray. Two inactive fault lines mark the border between the three zones. The Cape Ray Fault passes through J.T. Cheeseman Provincial Park just five kilometres north of Port aux Basques. Passing from the remains of the continental shelf of prehistoric Gondwanaland (Gander Zone), you will cross over to the Iapetus Ocean bed (Dunnage Zone).

Several kilometres further on, to the left, you will see three distinctive volcanic cones. These three-hundred-metre-high volcanoes were formed as the crust fractured and broke during the ancient collision of continents.

On the north side of the last volcanic cone, the Cabot Fault line crosses the highway at Featherbed Lake Brook. This fault marks the line between the Humber Zone and the Dunnage Zone. In effect, it separates the ancient Canadian Shield from what was the Iapetus Ocean bottom. The fault has been traced all the way to the Great Glen Fault in Scotland. The towering cliff face of the Long Range Mountains starts about four kilometres northwest of Cape Ray. This western-facing scarf of the mountain marks the line of the *Cabot Fault*. The volcanoes and the Table Land Mountains are a clue to the epochal events that took place here two hundred million years ago.

One must wonder what the Dorset Eskimos thought as they camped in the shadow of these extinct volcanoes. It is believed that these first human visitors arrived there in the last half of the first millennium B.C., crossing over a land bridge that existed between the south coast of Labrador and the Northern Peninsula. Over several centuries, they extended their range throughout most of the Island. While signs of their settlement have been found on the Great Northern Peninsula, archaeologists have discovered sites throughout northeastern Newfoundland and even on the south coast of the Island in Placentia Bay.

An important Dorset site was discovered at Cape Ray. Research indicates that these early native people established a spring hunting camp there and occupied it continuously for more than 800 years. That's twice as long as our own habitation of Newfoundland. Even with such a long period of occupation, the Dorset people managed to leave the island the same way as they had found it.

The Dorsets spent much of their year in small camps along the coast. Descended from Inuit peoples of the eastern Arctic, they were well suited for life in this harsh maritime environment. Like the Maritime Archaic people from 500 years before, the Dorsets main food source was the sea mammals that frequented the coast here. In the early spring, harp seals could be easily hunted from shore as they whelped their pups on the pan ice in the Gulf. Later in the spring and summer, the Dorset' supplemented their diet by catching plentiful salmon in local rivers. In the fall

147

and winter, they moved their camps further inland to pursue large herds of woodland caribou that migrated along the barren plateau atop the nearby Long Range Mountains. In the late winter, they would return again to Cape Ray.

Archaeologists believe that bands of thirty or forty people lived at Cape Ray. Their population peaked during the first half of the first millennium A.D. They lived on a rocky terrace at the very tip of the Cape. The long sandy beach just to the south of the camp permitted easy launching of their small kayaks.

Their houses were simple structures, built of poles and seal skins. The base of the house was set twelve inches into the ground, scalloped out of the turf down to the granite bedrock. A single square space about fifteen feet across contained the living space together with a sleeping platform. A rock-lined fire pit occupied the middle of the room, providing light and a heat source for cooking. Successive layers of wood ash and charcoal can still be found in the excavated fire pits. The dig at Cape Ray also revealed hundreds of chipped stone artifacts including spearheads and arrowheads, scrapers and tiny cutting blades. Even pieces of soapstone pots were found. The characteristics of these artifacts helped the researchers to identify the occupants as being Dorset in origin. After about 400 A.D., the culture disappeared from Newfoundland, supplanted perhaps by the precursors to the Beothuck Indians who remained in Newfoundland until after the first European settlement.

During Jacques Cartier's first voyage of discovery in the summer of 1534, he travelled down the west coast of Newfoundland. That fall, he rounded Cape Ray as he began his journey back to France. In the two centuries that followed, the west coast became the domain of seasonal French and Basques fishermen. The English concentrated their efforts on the eastern and northeastern portions of the Island.

At the beginning of the eighteenth century, the Queen Anne's War broke out between Britain and France. It dragged on for eleven years. In 1713, the Treaty of Utrecht proclaimed the end of the War. The terms of the Treaty, in part, forced the French to abandon all claim to Newfoundland, ceding to them instead Cape Breton Island. While the Treaty forbade French settlement in Newfoundland, it did recognize their historic fishing rights and permitted them to dry their catch on shore in the summer. These fishing and drying activities were restricted to an area which ran from Cape Bonavista to Point Riche half way down the Great Northern Peninsula. Fifty years later, at the end of the Seven Year's War, the northern boundary was shifted to the west to allow greater English control of the northeastern coast of the Island. The southern boundary was moved from Point Riche to Cape Ray. The Cape formed a natural boundary between the two areas of fishing activity, the west coast for the French and the south coast for the Americans and the English.

This unusual arrangement remained in place for another one hundred and fifty years. Each spring, countless fishermen would travel to snug harbours along the *French Shore*. The harbours had names like Port au Choix, La Scie, Port aux Basques, Baie Verte, Codroy and Port au Port. As the years passed, English and Scottish merchants, fishermen, farmers and loggers began to settle all along the west coast, hoping to exploit the rich resources there. The Colonial Government in St. John's began to feel that France's Treaty rights restricted their sovereign right to access the Island. In the last half of the nineteenth century, the Canadian Government took over the responsibility for managing the shipping lanes along the French Shore. This created a certain amount of rivalry between the two Governments.

By the end of the nineteenth century, the French were effectively crowded out of the area. For nearly a century, the French culture was slowly assimilated into the English and Scottish Newfoundland culture. Today it is seeing a rebirth along the Port au Port Peninsula near Stephenville. It is all that remains of three hundred years of French fishing activity on this part of the Island.

The Cabot Strait is a one-hundred-and-twenty-kilometre stretch of ocean that separates the southwest coast of Newfoundland from the northeast coast of Cape Breton Island. Ships travelling to and from ports on the St. Lawrence River must pass through this broad Strait. Mariners must contend with treacherous St. Paul's Island, located about one third of the way across the Strait on the Cape Breton side. Many captains would steer their ships to the east of St. Paul's Island, attempting to make the southwest coast of Newfoundland before adjusting their course for home. In that way, Cape Ray became a *landfall* for those who travelled through the Gulf of St. Lawrence. The problem was that the headland at Cape Ray was low. While the five-hundred-metre-high Long Range Mountains stood out clearly inland, the coastal lowland only reaches the modest elevation of thirty metres above sea level. Frequently hidden by dense sea fogs, this flat cape, together with the dozens of submerged reefs and low islands to the south, were the cause of some terrible shipwrecks.

Throughout the eighteenth century, there was considerable Naval traffic in the Gulf of St. Lawrence. The British Admiralty discovered early on, the danger associated with cutting too close to Cape Ray. In the summer of 1781, two ships departed out of Port Royal, the British stronghold in Jamaica. They were bound for Quebec City. Throughout that summer, there had been persistent rumours of a marauding fleet of French and Spanish warships terrorizing British shipping in the Caribbean. The Admiralty decided to send the sixteen gun sloop HMS

Duchess of Cumberland to accompany the merchantman *Venus*. The *Venus* was contracted to carry molasses, rum and other provisions to the British garrison at Quebec. On their trip north, the northeast flow of the Gulfstream drew the ships off course. Lost in a dense fog, both ships ploughed straight into a reef off Cape Ray. A heavy sea quickly crushed the wooden ships with the loss of all hands.

Fifty years later, an Irish emigrant ship was lost near Cape Ray with another huge loss of life. She was the *Lady Sherbrooke*. In late June 1831, the 380-ton ship departed from Londonderry with over three hundred and sixty passengers and crew crammed on board. The British and Irish emigrants were bound for Quebec to begin a new life in Canada. The *Lady Sherbrooke* made the east coast of Newfoundland safely. Captain Gambles intended to give the south coast of the Island a wide berth before turning his ship northward into the Gulf. Unfortunately, he turned the ship too soon; she went ashore at Mouse Island beside the little harbour at Channel near Port aux Basques. Three hundred and thirty people died in the chaotic sea at the base of the cliffs there.

By the mid nineteenth century, there were other activities taking place in the southwestern corner of the Island. Efforts to establish a telegraph line overland from Cape Race to Cape Ray began in 1851. Cape Ray was chosen as its western terminus because it was the closest point to Cape Breton. They originally intended to transfer messages across the Cabot Strait via steamer or even passenger pigeon. The "Newfoundland Electric Telegraph Company" commenced operations in 1853. Embroiled in controversy, bad financing and difficult conditions, it was not until the fall of 1886 before the line was completed right across the Island.

from *The Illustrated London News*, October 20, 1855

"Telegram terminus at Cape Ray, 1855, the volcanic cones can be seen in the background."

That same year, an attempt was made to lay a cable across the Strait. An engineer named MacKay was assigned the task of managing the project on board the SS *Bloodhound*. He wrote later, "It was found that Cape Ray cove, ten miles distant from Port aux Basques offered more facilities as a point of connection, besides being over five miles nearer to Cape North (Cape Breton). A frame telegraph house was put up, the telegraph instruments conveyed and a battery of 100 cups erected. Everything being thus prepared, the operation of laying the cable was commenced on Friday the 24th of August." They finished the link a few days later, completing the 1600 kilometre line that began at Cape Race, ran across the Island through to Cape Ray and then on to New York. Ironically, Cape Ray was chosen to receive another transmission cable from across Cabot Strait in 1990. It was a fibre optic cable linking Newfoundland to the rest of North America. This high-tech communications link is capable of handling thousands of phone calls per second, extending the "information highway" to Newfoundland.

Until the late 1840's, it appears that no one had considered building a lighthouse on the southwest coast of the Island. Given the growing marine traffic through the Cabot Strait and the number of spectacular accidents that took place in the area, this is surprising. This area of the Colony was in the grey zone between the two government jurisdictions. In 1860, Trinity House at Quebec City sent out their Chief Engineer, John Page, to begin surveying the entrance of the Gulf of St. Lawrence. His task was to recommend possible sites for the construction of lighthouses. During that summer, he visited the southwestern coast and recommended two possible sites. The first was Cape Anguille, thirty kilometres to the north of Cape Ray near the entrance to the Grand Codroy River. A second site was on Duck Island, a rocky islet about halfway between Cape Ray and Port aux Basques. When Inspector Oke found out, he would have nothing to do with the proposal. Oke wrote, "The Government of Canada are, no doubt, desirous to give vessels navigating the Gulf the benefit of an efficient light, on their approaching the neighbourhood of Cape Ray, and bound either to or from Quebec.....(but) placing a light on any one particular place on (this) coast is an impossibility." He reasoned that a lighthouse at Cape Anquille, located on the French Shore, would be too far to the northeast to be of any benefit to Newfoundland traffic on the south coast. Duck Island was quite inaccessible, making it very expensive to build and to maintain. He preferred a lighthouse at Channel Head at the entrance to Port aux Basques harbour. He was backed up by Captain John Orlebar, R.N., who was in charge of survey work for the Newfoundland Government at the time. "I beg to say that a Lighthouse on the coast, somewhere between the Island of Saint Pierre and Cape Ray, would be of great service to the trade of the British Provinces as well as to Newfoundland. I am of the opinion that a light on Channel Head would be of eminent service to the thriving settlement of Channel, and point out to strangers the locality of the excellent little harbour of Port aux Basques." Realizing that the Canadian Government would not agree to build two lighthouses in the area, Oke eventually agreed to the compromise of a lighthouse at Cape Ray, right on the boundary between Newfoundland's south coast fishing area and the French Shore. Lighthouses were eventually built at both Cape Anquille and Channel later in the century.

The final decision to build a lighthouse at Cape Ray, did not come for another five years. In the spring of 1870, the Privy Council of Canada resolved to carry out the work and wrote the Newfoundland Government, asking for their input. They curtly responded that it was part of the French Shore and therefore didn't really care where it went. The Federal Minister, Peter Mitchell, for the newly formed Department of Marine and Fisheries, wrote in his annual report, "It is proposed to build (the) new lighthouse of strong wooden frame tower, properly protected from the weather and although not so durable as stone lighthouse already built in the Gulf, and more liable to destruction by fire, still with proper precautions, it .... will assume all the purpose for which (it was) intended for many years to come." This decision to build a wooden lighthouse would be regretted fourteen years later.

Construction of the lighthouse and residence started that year, on the west side of the Cape about 650 feet from shore. They chose a granite knoll which was the highest point around. The tower was hexagonal in plan and was only nine feet in diameter, quite narrow compared to some of the more substantial Newfoundland lights. An iron lantern was placed at the top of the tower. Inside, a revolving catoptric lens contained twelve kerosene lamps complete with 20 inch reflectors. The project was completed the following summer at a cost of $11,350. The light was first exhibited on July 13, 1871.

Robert Rennie was appointed the first keeper at Cape Ray. He and his family moved into a substantial two storey residence. While the accommodations were first class, it seems that he was not very pleased with the design of the lighthouse tower. That first winter, it was racked by the incredibly heavy winds off the Gulf. Later in the century, this area of the province became well known, with stories of train locomotives being blown off the tracks. Rennie insisted that changes be made to the tower the next summer. After the work was completed he reported that, "the wire stays put on the tower, prevents it from shaking, and that the ventilators have been a great improvement to the ventilation and the lights (of the lantern)."

While the flashing light at Cape Ray would prove to be a steady guardian for the entrance to the Gulf of St. Lawrence, it did cause some confusion on the part of at least one captain passing its shore. Only two years after the completion of the light, in September, 1873, a Captain Corriveau sailed the 450 ton barque, *Rivoli* out of a harbour in Barbados, bound for Quebec with a cargo of molasses. Late on the evening of September 20, the *Revoli* approached the foggy southwestern coast of Newfoundland. Out of the fog, a lookout gleamed a faint light. Corriveau mistook the feeble light for the lighthouse at on St. Paul's Island fifty miles away to the west. He altered the *Revoli's* course to the east in an attempt to avoid the "island", only to run aground on a reef on a low rocky islet several kilometres south of Cape Ray. There off the island, the great ship hung. At dawn, a westerly gale sprang up and began to pound the ship to pieces. The heavy sea prevented the crew from getting a lifeboat off. On shore three local residents, realizing that the ship would soon break up, hurried to the scene. At great risk to their own lives, they managed to get a line to the stricken ship. Rigging a bosun's chair, the Captain and crew were safely transferred ashore. The survivors were taken to Channel and cared for by the residents until they could be returned home.

It was these cases of mistaken identity which the Department of Marine and Fisheries feared the most. Mariners had to be able to discern the difference between Cape Ray and St. Paul's in dense fogs. Plans had begun earlier that year to erect a fog alarm at Cape Ray. It was put into operation one month after the *Revoli* accident. So began a ten-year effort to find an effective fog alarm at the Cape Ray Station. The first alarm operated only five years. Eventually it was relocated at Point Amour because it "had proven of comparatively little service to shipping owing to its being placed in an unfavourable position."

In 1877, "A new, cheap and simple steam fog-horn owned by Mr. N.S. Woodward of Sherbrooke, Quebec (was) purchased by the Department and stationed at Cape Ray." It was operated by a smaller engine than normal, in hopes that it could be maintained at a smaller expense. Inspector Nevill did not appreciate the Woodward Fog Horn. He wrote, "These new alarms are of so small prime cost and are operated so economically that I hope (rather than expect) that they will prove effective." Nevill was quickly proven right for the fog horn did not last the winter. Rennie reported, "... its workings cannot be depended on, and it will be necessary to procure another horn or discontinue the one altogether at this station.... The fog horn has not worked well for some time; at first when it was put up it sounded well, but at present, it cannot be heard except at a short distance. The principle is not good, and I would recommend that a new one of a larger size be put (here) as soon as possible." A Neptune Fog Horn was installed in 1880, remaining there for the next thirty years.

The early 1880's would see some other important changes at the Cape Ray lighthouse station. Edward Rennie had been assisting his aging father. In October 1884, Robert Rennie retired, but not before he had arranged for a major renovation of the station. The renovation included a reconstruction of the tower with new clapboard being installed. Six months later, on April 1, 1885, the tower was destroyed by fire, "owing to the explosion of a lamp." The keeper's residence built some distance away from the tower was spared. Whether the accident had been the result of young Rennie's inexperience or simply a faulty lamp was never reported. The Department immediately arranged their supply vessel *Napoleon*, stationed in Montreal, to ferry materials and workmen to Cape Ray to replace the tower. Within four months, a new wooden lighthouse was completed on the same site. Inspector Nevill haughtily remarked in his annual report, "The wisdom of the course adopted here of using cast iron for Light towers has been illustrated by the destruction, by fire, of the wooden structure erected by the Dominion Government at Cape Ray. Wood is usually adopted because it is somewhat cheaper than iron; but one or two losses by fire would soon more than cover the difference of first cost for several stations. Further, iron is permanent, it may be said everlasting, and even requires less attention to painting than is required by perishable structures of wood."

In 1904, the Department constructed a marine radio station at Cape Ray, operated by the Marconi Wireless Telegraph Company, effectively eliminating the need for the telegraph cable terminal there. In 1907, the old steam horn was replaced by a compressed air diaphone. A new building to house the apparatus was built down at the very tip of the Cape.

"Keepers residence at Cape Ray."

The two World Wars passed uneventfully at the Cape Ray Station. In the late 1950's, Hiram Osbourne became the head keeper at the station. During those years, one of his assistants, Frank St. Croix, discovered a considerable number of stone arrowheads down below the

"Cape Ray Lighthouse"

lighthouse. Twenty years later, it would become the site of a major archaeological excavation.

In 1959, the old lighthouse tower burnt down for a second time. A year later, it was replaced on the same site with a new, rather uninspiring, reinforced concrete tower. An electric beacon was installed protecting a single 1000 W lamp. The old Victorian residence was demolished and replaced with several single-storey bungalows.

In the late 1970's, Gordon Thomas took over from Hiram Osburne who retired. The Cape Ray Lighthouse station was made automatic in the fall of 1991 when Thomas retired.

To get to the Cape Ray Lighthouse, follow the Trans Canada Highway fifteen kilometres northwestward from the Marine Atlantic Terminal at Port aux Basques. Watch for the access road to the J.T. Cheeseman Provincial Park. Beneath this park lies the ancient Cape Ray Fault. Continue on another kilometre or two watching for the first two volcanic cones. The paved road (Route 408) passes dramatically between these two cones, taking you down to the community of Cape Ray. The road will come to an intersection; take the right and turn across a small bridge. Drive out toward the beautiful two kilometre white sand beach that lies just beyond. The road bears off to the right along the low rocky headland that is the most southwestern point of the Island. As you come around the turn, you will see the Cape Ray Station low on the horizon.

Many of the original buildings have been removed in recent years. A fairly large bungalow remains, recently vacated by the last keeper, Gordon Thomas. Just behind this house on the hill you can still make out the outline of the original two-storey keeper's house. A short gravel road will take you down to the water's edge. On the left you may notice the foundations of the residences for an assistant keeper and the radio operator. Park beside the large one-and-a-half-storey fog alarm building built in 1907. Peeking through one of the high windows, you should make out the twin compressed air tanks used in the operation of the diaphone.

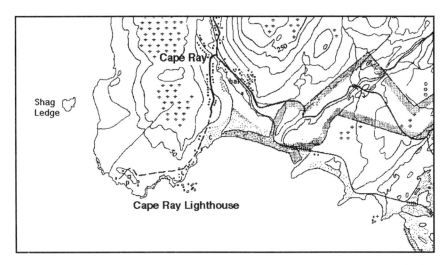

On your right, as you walk back up the gravel road toward the lighthouse, only fifty metres away, you should notice a narrow strip of grassy meadow. It runs like a ribbon along the pink and tawny granite cliffs above the sea. Just beyond is a large thicket of stunted black spruce reaching only a half metre in height. This thicket runs back up the hill to the lighthouse. It is this narrow grassy area where the archaeologists had discovered the Dorset eskimo camp. Rest awhile there on that grassy terrace. Look westward out toward the horizon, perhaps you will see one of the many large freighters that pass Cape Ray each day on their way to the great ports of North America and Europe.

Cape Norman
(Flash 0.5 seconds; eclipse 5.5 seconds)
The Norse Light

...Then they saw land and sailed to it,
and came to an island which lay to the north of the land.
They went to the highest point on that island to look around....
Afterward they went to their ship and sailed into a sound
that lay between the island and that cape which extended
to the north from the land. They steered in to the west of the cape.
It was very shallow there at ebb tide and their ship was grounded...
Yet they were so eager to go ashore
that they could not wait for the tide to rise under the ship....
They carried their sleeping bags ashore and built temporary shelters.
.... Later on, when they decided to remain there that winter,
they built a large house .... When spring came, they made ready and
sailed away.
Leif named the land for its products. He called it Vinland.

from *the Greenlander Saga*, circa 1385

For many centuries the *Greenlander Saga* was believed to be a mythical account of the travels of a family of Viking explorers. The stories were passed down from generation to generation until they were recorded in a manuscript in the fourteenth century. The original documents may be still seen today at the Royal Library in Copenhagen.

157

During the same period, several other Sagas appeared. These further corroborated the stories found in the Greenlander Saga. Together, they have been the subject of considerable scholarly research during the past century.

The Greenlander Saga begins with the story of the patriarch of the family, Eirik the Red. A rebel and a renegade, he was driven from his home in Norway after being found guilty of several counts of manslaughter. Eirik fled first to Iceland. A couple of years later, he was forced to leave Iceland for similar reasons. He sailed westward and rather than dropping off the face of the earth, Eirik the Red discovered a great glacier-covered island. Curiously enough, he named the place Greenland. It was there that he found sanctuary, establishing a colony on the southern tip of the great island. This cold and inhospitable place became home for himself and his family.

Leif, the eldest of four children, was raised on the stories of his father's exploits. He was particularly intrigued by the tales of lands that lay to the west of Greenland. Around 1000 AD, Leif sailed with thirty-five men and a small seaworthy ship in search of those fabled lands. He sailed westward across the Davis Strait, probably making his first landfall on the south coast of Baffin Island. This was a another cold, treeless place, full of high mountains and glaciers similar to his own homeland. Leif named it *Helluland* or "land of flat rocks". From there, Leif headed his ship southward along the coast of Labrador. He passed dense forests of spruce that ran down to rugged coastlines. In one place they noticed was a great sand beach. It is believed that the long beach described in the Saga may correspond to the area around Cape Porcupine on the coast of Labrador. He named this area *Markland* or "land of woods".

Leif continued another two days sailing southward from Markland, and finally reached his third landfall. On his right hand, the Labrador coast fell away to the west into what he must have thought was a great ice-filled fjord. This fjord was probably the Strait of Belle Isle. The Saga describes his brief landing on a large grass-covered island. From there he surveyed the Strait. Off to the southwest, he would have made out the tan-colored, limestone cliffs of Cape Norman - the northern tip of Newfoundland. Closer to Belle Isle he would have seen the high cliffs of Cape Bauld on Quirpoon Island.

Leif sailed his ship into a shallow, protected bay that lay along that shore. There just off the beach, the ship was grounded on rocks exposed at low tide. He and his men waded ashore to a grassy lowland that enclosed the small bay. A small river flowed down the hill into the bay.

Leif Eiriksson decided to establish an outpost in this site. He called the place *Vinland* after the wild grapes that were found nearby by one of his men. These "grapes" were probably the lowly blueberry (*Vac-

cinium angustifolium) that grows in great abundance throughout Newfoundland. Historians believe that the reference to wine and grapes may have been his attempt to attract Viking colonists to the place in much the same way that his father had named his bleak, icy island Greenland.

That winter, they built a long house there. It was constructed of grass sods and spruce timbers cut from the forest nearby. For these Greenlanders, the wood was considered a rare and valuable commodity. So they began to cut logs and stow them aboard the ship.

The Vikings feasted on the large salmon that filled the small river. Leif's men spread out across the barrens to forage for other food sources as well. The forest inland contained migrating herds of woodland caribou. In the spring, they travelled the twenty kilometres west along the coast to Pistolet Bay. Just beyond, on the tan limestone cliffs of Cape Norman, they could have hunted harp seals as they whelped their pups on the pan ice. In the spring, with their ship loaded with timber and "grapes", Lief Eiriksson and men sailed safely back to Greenland. This Viking settlement at Vinland is believed to be the first European habitation in North America.

The stories of the green meadows and the abundant resources must have stirred the Vikings in their frozen home, because Vinland was visited several times over the next ten years. Eirik's younger brother Thorvald spent a winter there, only to die in a skirmish with a band of either Dorset Eskimos or Beothuck Indians. The Vikings called them *Skraelings*. While the Vikings were ferocious warriors, in Vinland they were overwhelmed by the sheer numbers of attacking Indians.

A couple of years later, a Viking merchant named Thorfinn Karlsefni obtained permission to use Leif Eiriksson's outpost. Karlsefni hoped to establish a permanent settlement at Vinland. In 1008 AD, three ships entered that shallow bay on the northern tip of Newfoundland. They were loaded with one hundred and sixty Viking settlers including fifteen women. Also on board were cattle, sheep and an assortment of tools and equipment essential for their new life there. The settlers built several new long houses, and a series of storage buildings. During their first winter, a child was born to Gudrid and her husband Thorfinn Karlsefni. The boy's name was Snorri. He was the first European child to be born in North America.

The Vikings discovered deposits of naturally occurring iron ore beneath the bog. These "knuckles" of ore were heated in a crude forge that they had built at the edge of the settlement. In the red heat of the smelting forge, the iron fused together. It could be hammered into simple axes, adzes and knives.

The Skraelings returned to Vinland to trade furs for red wool cloth that the women had woven. Unfortunately, the bargaining did not go well and arguments started. Eventually, there was violence and both

Vikings and Indians died. At the end of their second winter, Karlsefni had had enough. They loaded their ships and returned to Greenland.

While there were one or two other attempts to settle the place, eventually the Vikings of Greenland lost interest in Vinland. At any rate, the Saga ends there. It appears that they never made another trip to the place. If it weren't for the Greenlander Saga and other stories, mankind would have forgotten about the Vikings' brief sojourn at Vinland. With the re-discovery of the Sagas in the nineteenth and twentieth centuries, archaeologists began to speculate about the existence of Vinland and its possible location. In 1960, the Norwegian archaeologist Helge Ingstad and his team found irrefutable evidence of a Viking settlement at L'Anse aux Meadows on the northern tip of Newfoundland.

The Strait of Belle Isle was left to the small bands of Beothuck Indians travelling along its shores in pursuit of migrating seals. It would remain so until the summer of 1534, when Jacques Cartier's small fleet entered the Strait - the first European ships in five hundred years. In the years that followed Cartier's discovery, the Strait of Belle Isle would become well known as Basque and Breton fishermen established whaling stations along these shores. Mariners recognized the high cliffs of *Cap Normand* as an excellent marker for the southeastern entrance to the Strait. It was probably one of these hardy Breton fishermen who named the cape after their distant home in northern France - Normandy.

The shortest route between ports in Europe and those on the St. Lawrence River is through the Strait of Belle Isle. Nevertheless, in the eighteenth and early nineteenth centuries, sailors avoided the Strait. They chose to travel south of Newfoundland, entering the Gulf of St. Lawrence through the much wider Cabot Strait. The Strait of Belle Isle is completely filled with ice for at least half of the year. During the remainder of the year, they had to contend with strong currents, menacing icebergs, dense fogs and constantly shifting winds in the relatively long, narrow passage.

With the advent of steamships, more and more traffic began to use the Strait in the summer months. In the mid nineteenth century, with the rise in trade between Britain and Europe and North America, more and more people and goods had to cross the Atlantic Ocean. It was a period of considerable competition between the various shipping lines hoping to capitalize on this demand. They chose the "short cut" through the treacherous Strait of Belle Isle, hoping to reduce their time at sea.

In 1855, Point Amour lighthouse was built on the south coast of Labrador. It would light the northwestern entrance to the Strait of Belle Isle. Three years later, in 1858, Quebec Trinity House ordered the construction of a lighthouse on the southern end of Belle Isle. Belle Isle is the large fifteen square mile island that lies off the northern tip of

Newfoundland. Belle Isle is possibly the grass covered island mentioned in Leif Eirikson's first visit to Vinland. The lighthouse there marked the northeastern entrance to the Strait, aiding ships entering from the North Atlantic.

Even with these lighthouses marking the entrances of the Strait, the presence of spring pack ice made crossings very risky. Mariners who used the Strait before the end of June, did so at their own peril.

Those on board the SS *Canadian* made such a mistake. The passenger liner *Canadian* was owned by the Quebec & Liverpool Line. She arrived at Quebec City in late May 1861, loaded with families headed for Western Canada. On June 1, she departed again on her return trip to Liverpool. Luckily, she did not carry the hundreds of passengers who occupied her cabins only weeks before.

On the evening of June 3, the ship arrived off the south coast of Labrador stopping to consult with the lighthouse keeper at Point Amour. Monsieur Blampied reported that there had been heavy pack ice in the Strait all week. Captain Graham prudently decided to anchor his ship there until morning. He knew that any attempt to make the passage through the Strait at night would be foolhardy. During the night, weather conditions deteriorated. In the dim light of dawn, the ship was tossed before huge swells that had been built up by gale force southerly winds. Heavy rains dashed against the glass on the bridge as Captain Graham gave the order to get the liner underway. The *Canadian* slowly proceeded northeast through the Strait. She had to force her way through the heavy pan ice, dodging enormous icebergs on all sides. The ship had to buck a stiff ocean current, speeding through the Strait at four knots.

By 10 o'clock in the morning, the *Canadian* had made it as far as Cape Norman. Across from those bare, tan cliffs, the liner came upon a heavily packed icefield. The pack was so thick that the ship was unable to penetrate it. Captain Graham ordered the ship slowed. He hoped that they could hold their position until the pack ice loosened up enough to continue on to the open sea. The *Canadian* managed to hold there for nearly two hours; great pieces of ice pounded and shook the ship as they slowly ground by. Then, at 11:35 am, she was struck by one piece of ice which tore a huge gash in the hull below the waterline.

The *Canadian* began to settle quickly. Captain Graham did not relish the thought of going down in the middle of the ice-filled Strait. He ordered full speed for Cape Norman, hoping to get the *Canadian* ashore before she went down. The attempt was futile. Gripped in the ice, it quickly became clear that the ship was not going to make it before she sank. The engines were stopped and the order was given to abandon ship. The crew began the process of transferring passengers into the lifeboats. All the boats managed to get away safely except for the

Number 8 Lifeboat. Heavily loaded, the boat capsized in the rough sea as it was being released from the ship's lines. All thirty-five passengers and crew aboard died in the icy water. The *Canadian* went down quickly with the last lifeboat getting away only five minutes before she sank.

Fishermen from the nearby community of Quirpoon witnessed the accident. Quickly, they got several small rescue boats out to the place where the *Canadian* had gone down. They guided the lifeboats back to Quirpoon. The survivors were kept there in the fishermen's homes until they could be safely transported to St. John's later in the spring.

Marine traffic in the Strait of Belle Isle continued to grow in the 1860's. This fact was not missed by Trinity House in Quebec City. After Confederation in 1867, the newly formed Department of Marine and Fisheries made it a priority to improve the situation in the Straits. The Minister of the day, Hon. Peter Mitchell, indicated in his 1869 report to the House of Commons, "I have also brought under the notice of my colleagues, the urgent necessity which exists in the River and Gulf of St. Lawrence, *the great highway to the West,* for additional lights with a view of facilitating the general Trade and Commerce of the Dominion...."

Two years later, the Privy Council of Canada gave approval to build a wooden lighthouse at Cape Norman. They chose the highest point of the Cape, at the edge of a sheer one-hundred-and-ten-foot cliff. The site commanded a spectacular view up and down the Strait. The tower was built by the Department of Public Works at a cost of $10,157.00. The design was similar to the first tower at Cape Ray built at the same time. Hexagonal in plan, it stood 35 feet high and was 17 feet in diameter at the base.

"Cape Norman Lighthouse"

The iron lantern placed at the top of the tower was painted white with a red roof. It contained a revolving catoptric lens housing six circular wick lamps. These oil lamps were installed in a frame together with their 20 inch reflectors. The entire lens assembly rotated at a rate

162

of one revolution every two minutes, powered by a system of weights that ran the length of the tower.

Mitchell reported that, "Mr. Henry Locke, a resident of that locality, who has been highly recommended to me, was placed as keeper at a salary of $500 per annum." He and his family moved into a modest residence which was built across from the lighthouse. It appears that Locke encountered some difficulties with the design of the lighthouse within two years of its completion. The light was reported out throughout the winter of 1873 and the spring of 1874. While problem was never explained, six wire stays were attached to the lighthouse later that year to steady it. It appears that the tower had been designed too lightly to withstand the hurricane force winds that funnelled though the Strait in the winter.

While being highly visible from the sea, the decision to locate these lighthouses on the highest point did have its disadvantages, as a neighbouring lighthouse keeper on Belle Isle would discover a couple of years later. It would seem that Martin Coltin and his family had an even quieter life at the Belle Isle Station than at a mainland station. Even Henry Locke would welcome visits from the inhabitants of nearby Boat Harbour and Cook's Harbour. A freak accident of nature shattered Coltin's quiet life in 1876. The Department would report later, "At half-past nine on the night of August 9, 1876, the tower and dwelling house were struck by lightning, tearing off clapboards on both sides of the tower, and smashing the frame and door. (It) also ran down the lightning rod, entered the roof of the dwelling house and passed through the upper and lower floor at both sides of the house, tearing them to pieces and doing them considerable damage. It also entered the stable and killed a goat and dog. The keeper and one of his family were considerably injured. Carpenters will be sent down this fall by the steamer *Napoleon* to repair the damages and also fix up extra lightning rods." Given the violence of the lightning strike, Coltin and his family were lucky to get away with their lives.

The year before Henry Locke retired, a major accident took place out in the Strait that would affect the development of facilities at the Cape Norman Lighthouse Station in years to come. The 2,160 ton steamship *Montreal* was on a voyage from Montreal to Liverpool, her holds filled with cattle and general cargo. Only ten years old, she was the pride of her owners - the Dominion Steamship Company.

The Captain intended to navigate the *Montreal* up the midstream of the Strait, making for Cape Norman. He knew that from there a course due east would carry the ship straight out into the North Atlantic, allowing them to safely clear the south end of Belle Isle. Unfortunately, things did not work out exactly as they had planned. On the morning of August 4, 1889, the *Montreal* entered the west entrance of the Strait near Point Amour. They were greeted with a troublesome sight - a dense sea fog that had enveloped the entire Strait area. They would be forced to use dead reckoning in order to proceed. Out of the early morning darkness, great bergs loomed. The Captain was forced to constantly alter course to avoid those mountains of ice. They did not realize that a strong easterly current was drawing the ship further out into midstream away from the guiding light of Cape Norman and toward Belle Isle. Nor did they hear the warning shots of the fog gun firing from the heights of Belle Isle. Lost in the dense fog, the ship went ashore there, and became a total loss in the heavy sea. Fortunately, no lives were lost, as the passengers and crew were safely taken off before the ship broke up.

In an inquiry later, the officers were exonerated of any wrongdoing. It was felt that had there been a fog horn at Cape Norman, the accident could have been avoided. The following year, the Department built a steam fog horn three hundred feet to the east of the lighthouse on the very cliff face overlooking the water. Forty-seven year old, John Cambell was the contractor on site. After completing the building and installing the equipment, he stayed on to operate the fog station. Later that year, after Locke retired, John Cambell became the head keeper; his descendants still keep the lighthouse at Cape Norman today.

In 1892, Dr. Wilfred Grenfell came to the area as a medical missionary, sponsored by the Mission to Deep Sea Fishermen of Britain. Travelling in a small boat he visited the fishing communities along the Great Northern Peninsula and the south coast of Labrador. He was appalled by the living conditions of the fishermen and native peoples and dedicated his life to their well being. Dr. Grenfell established a hospital at St. Anthony and a nursing station at Battle Harbour on the coast of Labrador.

Over the next several decades, Dr. Grenfell tried to improve the lives of the people who lived along this coast. He did so in a direct way as a medical doctor, but also indirectly by encouraging cooperation and local entrepreneurship with a dash of Christian life thrown in for good measure. In order to finance his work on the northern coast, Dr. Grenfell wrote numerous books on his life there, for the British and American public. He went on wide-ranging lecture tours to further publicize his work with the *Grenfell Mission* as it came to be known. His efforts were very successful. By the time he died in 1940, the Grenfell Mission had become the main provider of health and social services in northern Newfoundland and Labrador.

The little wooden lighthouse at Cape Norman did not survive the powerful winds of the Strait of Belle Isle. The frail design allowed considerable movement in the tower which in turn risked putting the light mechanism out of kilter. Given the importance of this light to shipping in the Strait, the Department of Marine and Fisheries decided to replace the light in 1907. They ordered a "segmental cast iron tower" for Cape Norman. It was fabricated in Quebec at a cost of $12,839.25. Beyond the fact that it would be much more durable, the tower was nearly twenty feet higher than the wooden one. The extra height meant that the new lighthouse could be seen as far as sixteen miles away. The iron tower was built beside the original tower on the bluff overlooking the Strait. The old wooden tower was taken down to the first floor and roofed over for use as a storehouse.

The Department replaced the revolving light mechanism after the recent installation of a double flashing light at nearby Cape Bauld. Cape Norman's light characteristics were too similar to this neighbouring light. The Department acquired a third order triple flashing apparatus from Seal Island, Nova Scotia. Cape Norman's old light mechanism was sent to the lighthouse station at Matane, Quebec. This new fixture included finely crafted kerosene vapour lamps built by the firm of Barber, Bernard et Turenne of Paris, France.

The old steam fog alarm was replaced the following year. The new alarm with a three inch diaphone was installed in a new building just to the east of the original fog alarm. That same year, a fine, two storey duplex residence for the keeper and his assistant was also built just below the lighthouse.

John Cambell spent only a few years in the new keeper's house before he passed away at the age of sixty-eight years. His eldest son, Alex, took over as the head keeper at Cape Norman in 1911. He was thirty-seven years old at the time, and would remain in the position until he retired just before World War II.

"New residence at Cape Norman"

The design of the new iron tower was faulty. In the late 1920's, it had to be encased in a protective shell of concrete. The tower was further supported using a system of flying buttresses. This structural detail was developed by Lieutenant Colonel William Anderson. Anderson was the Chief Engineer for the Department of Marine and Fisheries at the time. Six wedge-shaped concrete struts extended from the top of the tower at a steep angle down to the base. While they were only twelve inches in diameter, each buttress was able to strengthen the tower from a different angle. The design was similar to several other lighthouses built by Anderson. The lighthouse built on the north side of Belle Island in 1905 had a similar design.

On one cold foggy morning in June 1937, the 3900 ton tanker SS *Kyno* almost met her end on the jagged cliffs of Cape Norman. Owned by Bowring Brothers, the ship carried bulk oil from ports in Britain to a refinery in Montreal. In mid June, she had departed from Scotland for the two week Atlantic crossing. For some unknown reason, the Captain and crew never heard the fog alarm sounding high on the cliffs of Cape Norman until it was too late. The ship grounded amidships on the limestone reef that lies just off the Cape. She hung there as the heavy seas began to break over her. The crew abandoned the ship, escaping by lifeboat to the safety of the nearby shore. Luckily, the strong westerly winds abated, and the steel tanks holding the oil did not puncture. The tug *Lord Strathcona* was dispatched from Montreal and arrived on the scene four days after the accident. They managed to patch up the tanker and then safely pulled her off the reef. Under tow, the *Kyno* eventually arrived in Montreal.

During World War II, young Jacob Cambell took over from his father Alex, who was retiring. During those war years, the young keeper would sit up in the old iron lantern and watch as Canadian destroyers scurried urgently in and out of the Strait on unknown missions. Convoys of freighters and cargo ships ferrying supplies for the European war would slip unseen through the Strait under cover of darkness.

"Aerial photo of Cape Norman station by Lee Wulff"

courtesy of Public Archives, Newfoundland & Labrador

In the1950's, the Department of Transportation decided to replace the concrete and iron tower. The mortar in the concrete buttresses, exposed to the ravages of salt ocean spray, had begun to rot. The pillars loosened by the rotten joints began to move in the ever present wind. In 1963, the tower was replaced with a new concrete structure. A ten-foot-wide aluminium lantern at the top held a single 110V 400W Mercury Vapour lamp in a D3 panel lens. Alvin Cambell took over from his father Jacob, who passed away in 1984. Alvin Cambell is the fourth generation of the Cambell family to keep the light at Cape Norman. He operates the lighthouse today.

To get to Cape Norman, you must travel along the same route that you would take to reach Point Amour. Starting at Deer Lake on the Trans Canada Highway, follow the Viking Trail (Route 430) westward to the coast at Gros Morne National Park. The site for this National Park was chosen in part because of the spectacular geology of its ancient mountains and steep-sided fjords. Follow the Viking Trail northward along the west coast of Newfoundland. You will be driving on a coastal lowland which was submerged twelve million years ago by the enormous weight of glacial ice. On your right, the two-thousand-foot-high Long Range Mountains continue northeastward, having started far to the southwest at Cape Ray. They are the vestiges of the ancient Appalachian Mountain Range created during the continental collision 400 million years ago. You cannot help but notice the distinctive U-shaped valleys carved out of these high mountains. These valleys were formed by the grinding action of the great glacier iceflows to the sea.

As you drive up the coast of the Great Northern Peninsula, you will notice the sea-smoothed shapes of limestone. These formations were created from the calcareous remains of early marine organisms. They were deposited in the warm clear water of the coastal margin of that ancient continent, Laurentia. Today, if you walk along these limestone shelves, you may still see at your feet the imprints of pre-Cambrian trilobites and the swirling shells of early molluscs.

The drive up the Viking Trail from Deer Lake to the turnoff road for Cape Norman is approximately 450 kilometres. As you catch your first glimpse of wide, shallow Pistolet Bay, watch for Route 435, on your left. It is only a few kilometres beyond to the turnoff for L'Anse aux Meadows National Historic Park (Route 436). The drive to the regional centre at St. Anthony will take another fifteen minutes.

Route 435 will take you northward to the Strait of Belle Isle. Drive along a landscape which consists of water-filled bogs interspersed with numerous small ponds and low thickets of black spruce. Pistolet Bay on your right is dotted with a multitude of round boulders, deposited ten million years ago as the glaciers receded from this area. The dirt road has its share of pot holes but is quite passable, allowing you to drive at seventy or eighty kilometres per hour.

Twenty-five kilometres from the Viking Trail junction, you will come to the intersection with the road into Cook's Harbour. This fishing community is built around a sheltered harbour at the entrance to Pistolet Bay. It is oriented northwards, toward the dark coast of Labrador on the horizon. The houses of the village come down to the water's edge. Ice pans fill the harbour even in July. Cape Onion lies to the east of the bay. Just beyond is another shallow bay where the Greenland Vikings landed nearly one thousand years ago.

Instead of driving into Cook's Harbour, turn left to drive the last few kilometres to Cape Norman. If it isn't foggy, you should see the lighthouse on the horizon. Just past the tiny hamlet of Wild Bight, you will come to a "T" intersection. Turn right here and head out toward the limestone cliffs that rise up at the edge of the sea. As you pass the local dump, the majestic panoramic view of the Strait of Belle Isle opens up - you have reached the very northern tip of Newfoundland. This is a wild, treeless place, a landscape featureless except for a lone abandoned house, standing like a grey sentinel at the entrance to the sea cliffs. As the road takes a sharp turn to the left, you will notice a small cemetery where three generations of Cambells are buried.

Park in the small parking lot beside the fog alarm building. This is the first building, the one with the large red compressed air tank outside. From this vantage, it is clear why the Strait is known as "Iceberg Alley". Most of the year, you can witness the silent passage of dozens of magnificent icebergs through the Strait. Later in the summer and fall, the Strait becomes the "great highway to the west" as it was once described. Today, hundreds of ships use the Strait to access the port cities on the St. Lawrence River.

Looking to the northeast, you may see the outline of Belle Isle. There, two historic lighthouses still operate. It is fairly narrow across the Strait here. Looking to the north northwest, you will just make out the community of Red Bay on the Labrador side of the Strait. An early Basque whaling station operating in the sixteenth century was discovered at Red Bay in the 1970's.

Be careful, for just beyond the lighthouse the cliff drops straight down one hundred and ten feet to a smooth flat limestone ledge. The cliff is hidden and there are no guardrails. It poses quite a hazard to young children and anyone who is not watching for the precipice.

The reinforced concrete lighthouse is located on the highest point of the Cape. A modern one-and a half-storey keeper's residence is located just across from the lighthouse. Beyond the present tower, you can see the shells of two abandoned bungalows which must have housed the

168

assistant keepers and their families in years gone by. Interestingly, you can still see the outline of the iron tower built on the spot in 1907. When they dismantled this tower in the 1960's, they simply cut through the iron plate at its juncture with the concrete base. Beside the remains of the 1907 tower, you may notice six iron anchors in a hexagonal plan. These are the anchors for the wire stays that were installed to stabilize the original wooden tower in 1874.

One final hazard should be mentioned about this site. It is a menace, which has had as an unusual consequence: allowed some of the rarest flora to grow in eastern North America. The existence of exotic orchids at Cape Norman has drawn botanists from around the world. The upper surface of the limestone upon which the lighthouse is built is not smooth like the sea ledge below. Rather, the softer surfaces of the rock have been etched by hundreds of millions of years of weathering. It has produced a broken landscape of jagged projections interspersed with narrow troughs about twelve inches deep. **The unique surface makes it very difficult to walk on, especially for the young or the old. To move around, you must take broad steps from projection to projection. It is easy to stumble and fall on those pointed shards of limestone**.

This unusual geological formation has produced the ideal micro-climate for beautiful calcium-loving sub-Arctic orchids. The soil created at the bottom of these rock indentations has a high pH. This characteristic is very different from the more common, highly acidic soils of the island. The shallow troughs protect the flowers from the constant chill winds. A visitor exploring the terrain around Cape Norman may stumble across numerous varieties of orchids. Most notable is *Platanthera albida* var. *straminea*. This small plant with its elliptic, shiny green leaves and tiny cluster of flowers is actually an Eurasian species which has its western most distribution in the Cape Norman region. It is found nowhere else in North America. The little yellow-green flowers grow in a crowded group attached to the tip of the main stem. Their arrangement is similar to the common garden variety of Lily-of-the-Valley. The distinctive lower petal, referred to as the lip, has three petals. If you are lucky enough to find an example of *Platanthera abibda* var. *straminea*, smell it, for it gives off a strong vanilla-like fragrance.

Another dwarf orchid named *Amerorchis rotundifolia* thrives on the cool, moist, lime-rich soil that accumulates in these shallow depressions. It flowers in June and July. This orchid usually has a single elliptic leaf. A cluster of delicate pink-white flowers crown a single stalk. The large lip is speckled with tiny red-purple spots.

The yellow lady's-slipper *Cypripedium calceoulus* var. *planipetalum* is unique because unlike other yellow lady's-slippers, the lateral petals of this form are short and untwisted. This orchid is named for its

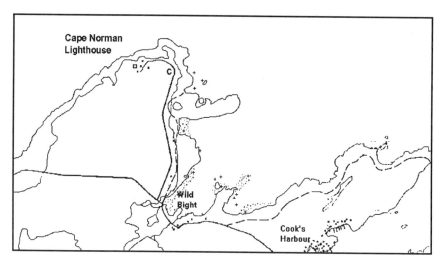

distinctive, yellow pouch at the bottom of the flower. This rare form is found only in isolated areas of western and northern Newfoundland and the north shore of Quebec. This beautiful, dwarf orchid flowers in July.

One final orchid that you should watch for is the little "frog orchid", *Coeloglossum virde* var. *virde*. Tiny green flowers cluster along a central stalk. It got its name because the long lip is forked or has a "hollow tongue". The plant is very small; its flowers blend in well with the wild grasses that grow in the depressions.

These very brief descriptions are taken from an excellent book of the subject, *Native Orchids of the United States and Canada*, by Carlyle Luer. He also mentions several other dwarf orchids that grow at Cape Norman including *Platanthera hyperborea*, *Platanthera obtusata*, *Platanthera hookeri*, *Malaxis monophyllos*, and *Arethusa bulbosa*.

These tiny, delicate orchids are easily missed unless you search carefully along the top of this broken limestone cape. **Carry a camera and try to photograph one of these very rare plants, but please do not pick them**. These orchids propagate by seed; flowers form so infrequently and the conditions are so severe that any reduction in the number of seeds may mean the collapse of their population. Look up as you search along the cliff, in the distance, you will see the Cape Norman lighthouse as it flashes its guiding light for those who make passage through the ice-strewn Strait of Belle Isle.

Epilogue

In the months since we completed the manuscript for this book, it seems that the public's interest in historic lighthouses has grown. A multi-million dollar Tourism Agreement was signed last year between the Provincial and Federal Governments. A portion of these funds have gone toward the restoration of the Point Amour Lighthouse and keepers residence on the Straits of Labrador. Under this same agreement, the access road to Cape St. Mary's has been upgraded and a new Interpretation Centre will be constructed adjacent to the lighthouse there. The Historic Resources Division continues to develop new exhibits at the Cape Bonavista Lighthouse and preparations are well underway for the 500th anniversary of John Cabot's landfall at Cape Bonavista in 1997.

The Ferryland Historical Society is seeking funding to restore the keepers residence at Ferryland Head. Recently, the Society rejected an offer for a "make work" project because the bureaucracy refused to consider their application to halt the destruction of the keepers residence and begin the process of restoring the lighthouse site. The residents of Cape Ray have formed their own Historical Society, their goal is to restore the Cape Ray Lighthouse Station. Similar efforts are underway just north in the Codroy Valley for the development of the lighthouse site at Cape Anguille. The people of Rose Blanche, an outport community southeast of Port aux Basque hope to restore the magnificent, granite lighthouse ruins abandoned at the entrance to their harbour in the 1940's.

Archaeologists worked on the "Southside Castle" site on the shores of the Narrows in St. John's harbour this past summer. It is just a "stones throw" from Fort Amherst lighthouse. Archaeological work has taken place at the George Calvert's settlement beside the "pool" in Ferryland harbour. Over the past two summers, many students and townsfolk from Ferryland have been trained by Dr. Jim Tuck from Memorial University to work the site. They are now carefully unearthing the artifacts left by their own ancestors three hundred and seventy years ago.

We can touch the roots of our maritime past by understanding what happened at these worn iron and stone lighthouses. Many original lighthouses have been lost as governments, streamlining the system of navigational aids, have abandoned them for unmanned skeleton towers. But many more can still be saved and be celebrated if the efforts of these community groups be encouraged. This was the goal of our book - to chronicle the history of our most significant lighthouses. There are several hundred lighthouses ringing the coasts of this province. They all have their own stories to tell. These stories weave through our folklore. This rich cultural heritage makes our province unique. Perhaps, these stories may stir the reader in whatever place in our country, to find out more about their own historic buildings and work to preserve them for their children.

The men and women who lived and worked in these beautiful, wild places are gone but we can still be touched by them through that transparent veil of time.

David Molloy
St. John's, Newfoundland
March 1, 1994

PRINTED IN CANADA